THE MANY FACES OF
FAMILY VIOLENCE

THE MANY FACES OF FAMILY VIOLENCE

Edited by

JERRY P. FLANZER, D.S.W.

With

Barbara Star, Ph.D.
Kathryn Conroy, C.S.W.
Jerry P. Flanzer, D.S.W.
John J. Steffen, Ph.D.
Mark Krain, Ph.D.
Robert Sarver, J.D.
Janet Rosenzweig-Smith, M.S., A.C.S.E.
Riley Regan, M.S.W., M.P.H.
Gisela Spieker, Ph.D.

CHARLES   C   THOMAS   •   PUBLISHER
Springfield • Illinois • U.S.A.

Published and Distributed Throughout the World by
CHARLES C THOMAS • PUBLISHER
2600 South First Street
Springfield, Illinois 62717, U.S.A.

© *1982 by* CHARLES C THOMAS • PUBLISHER

ISBN 0-398-04612-3

Library of Congress Catalog Card Number: 81-16722

*With THOMAS BOOKS careful attention is given to all details of
manufacturing and design. It is the Publisher's desire to present books that are
satisfactory as to their physical qualities and artistic possibilities and
appropriate for their particular use. THOMAS BOOKS will be true to those
laws of quality that assure a good name and good will.*

Printed in the United States of America
I-RX-1

HQ
809.3
U5
M36
1982

Library of Congress Cataloging in Publication Data
Main entry under title:

The Many faces of family violence.

   Bibliography: p.
   Includes index.
   Contents: Introduction / Jerry P. Flanzer — Patterns
in family violence / Barbara Star — Long-term treatment
issues with battered women / Kathryn Conroy — [etc.]
   1. Family violence — United States — Addresses, es-
says, lectures. I. Flanzer, Jerry P. II. Star, Barbara.
[DNLM: 1. Family. 2. Family therapy. 3. Violence.
HQ 809 M294]
HQ809.3.U5M36   362.8'2   81-16722
ISBN 0-398-04612-3   AACR2

ABOUT THE AUTHORS

INTRODUCTION by Jerry P. Flanzer, D.S.W. Dr. Flanzer, an associate professor of the Graduate School of Social Work at the University of Arkansas at Little Rock, served from 1978-81 as director of the Mid-America Institute on Violence in Families and from 1978-82 as director of the Arkansas Alcohol/Child Abuse Demonstration Project.

CHARACTERISTICS OF FAMILY VIOLENCE by Barbara Star, Ph.D. Dr. Star is an associate professor at the School of Social Work at the University of Southern California, Los Angeles. An original advisory board member for Mid-America, she was the recipient of a grant from the Levi Strauss Foundation to conduct a national study on shelters for battered women.

LONG-TERM TREATMENT ISSUES WITH BATTERED WOMEN by Kathryn Conroy, C.S.W. Ms. Conroy is director of the Park Slope Program of the Sisters of Good Shepherd in Brooklyn. She is also a member of the faculty of Hunter College, New York.

ALCOHOL AND FAMILY VIOLENCE by Jerry P. Flanzer.

SOCIAL COMPETENCE, FAMILY VIOLENCE AND PROBLEM DRINKING by John J. Steffen, Ph.D. Dr. Steffen is an associate professor with the Department of Psychology at the University of Cincinnati. He is coauthor with Dr. Paul Karoly of *Improving the Long-Term Effects of Psychotherapy* and is in the process of publishing a series entitled *Advances in Child Behavior, Analysis and Therapy*, also with Dr. Karoly. The first two volumes were scheduled to be released in late 1981.

A SOCIOLOGICAL PERSPECTIVE ON THE CONTROL OF VIOLENCE IN FAMILIES by Mark Krain, Ph.D. Dr. Krain is an associate professor of gerontology at the University of Arkansas at Little Rock. He has written in the area of interpersonal relationships and the family and has done needs assessments for community agencies in the area of personal relations and the family. He is currently writing a book on gerontology.

PROGRAMS FOR ASSAULTERS: Nationwide Trends by Barbara Star.

THE REMEDIES: Rhetoric or Reality? by Robert Sarver, J.D. Mr. Sarver holds joint appointments with the Graduate School of Social Work and the University of Arkansas Law School. He was first commissioner for corrections for the state of Arkansas and served as director of the correctional facilities of the state of West Virginia. He frequently serves as an expert consultant regarding correctional facilities across the United States.

HUMAN SEXUALITY CONCERNS IN THE TREATMENT OF CHILD SEXUAL ABUSE AND INCEST by Janet Rosenzweig-Smith, M.S., A.C.S.E. Ms. Rosenzweig-Smith was the project co-director of the Knoxville Institute for Sexual Abuse Training, funded by the National Center on Child Abuse and Neglect, and part of Knoxville's Child and Family Services. She was co-founder of a shelter.

ALCOHOL PROBLEMS AND FAMILY VIOLENCE: A Message to the Helpers by Riley Regan, M.S.W., M.P.H. Mr. Regan is director of the Division of Alcoholism of the Department of Public Health for the state of New Jersey. He is also national president of the Association of State Alcoholism and Drug Abuse Directors. He serves as cochairman of the steering committee to develop the NIAAA five-year plan and is on the board of directors of the Halfway House alcoholism program.

EPILOGUE by Gisela Spieker, Ph.D. Dr. Spieker is a professor of the Graduate School of Social Work at the University of Arkansas at Little Rock. During 1981-82 she served as acting dean. A founding member of the Mid-America Institute, she has also served as president of the Lutheran Social Services of Arkansas.

ACKNOWLEDGMENTS

This book represents select presentations given at national symposia on family violence conducted annually from 1978 through 1980 in Hot Springs by the Mid-America Institute on Violence in Families. The Institute, a component of the Graduate School of Social Work, University of Arkansas at Little Rock, was funded to a large extent by the Levi Strauss Foundation. With the support of the GSSW and UALR faculty and a network of professionals around the country, the Institute has been able to help generate clinical research, provide limited technical articles, but above all train hundreds of professionals from around the nation and even a few from overseas.

Specific acknowledgment must be given to Fred A. Morrow, Ph.D., Dean of the graduate School of Social Work, UALR, and a primary founder and motivator of the Institute, and to Phyllis Brandon, administrative assistant to the Institute and assistant editor to this manuscript. Without their assistance, the assistance of the many contributors, outside experts, faculty and staff, and the Institute, this manuscript would not have been possible.

CONTENTS

THE MANY FACES OF
FAMILY VIOLENCE

Chapter 1

INTRODUCTION

Jerry P. Flanzer

We continue to survive in a violent world. The nature of this violence in our society, as exhibited by wars and urban riots, appears to be more horrible and ghastly than ever. We also continue to survive in and among violent families. Although we are increasingly aware of the abuse among family members, no new information exists to prove that the nature of family life, although excessively violent, is any more brutal than it has been for centuries. "What constitutes violence is always a social construction. Acts of violence which are deemed legitimate are characterized as means of control or punishment . . . The line between socially acceptable force and illegitimate violence is thus a thin one."[1]

Freeman's statement is a telling one. As soon as society begins to lower its limits as to what is acceptable aggression within the family structure, family violence, as presently constituted, should begin to subside. In fact, it is this writer's belief (and hope) that as shame of family violence achieves societal awareness, the amount of physical beatings and emotional neglect within today's family structures will actually decrease. Therefore, the necessity of publications such as this one is evident.

Despite a possible lessening of the problem, all forms of vio-

lence in families do exist today and are still accompanied by staggering statistics. This chapter takes a quick glimpse at the prevalence (the next chapter gives more detailed descriptions and definitions) and then looks at the question: Why now? Why the
issue of family violence at the present time? And, finally, after
delving into the family systems approach's contribution to understanding family violence, provides the needed background to understanding the chapters that follow.

PREVALENCE OF FORMS OF FAMILY VIOLENCE

Violence can take many forms among family members. Each
pairing within the family system has the built-in potential for conflict, physical abuse, and/or emotional neglect. Thus, parent-to-
parent (spouse abuse), child-to-child (sibling abuse), or child-to-
parent (parent abuse or "granny bashing") abuses potentially
exist as a fertile ground for sowing family violence. These types
of violence may vary from direct hitting/battering to sexual abuse
and exploitation to severe physical/emotional neglect—all secreted
within the confines of the family. Generally, violent episodes
among and between family members are usually not single incidents. Most frequently, family violence is an intense, recurrent
act—one that will continue and may even escalate unless an external outside intervention emerges to prevent or deter its prog-
ress.
Family violence occurs among all ages of socioeconomic, ethnic,
and racial groups, although its existence among wealthier and
dominant groups tends to be less visible to public scrutiny. Estimates of incidence are of necessity "guesstimates" (author's ter-
minology), because perpetrators of abuse and their victims are
often reluctant to report this type of problem. The following
helps to illustrate this situation.
Investigators have found a high proportion of victim-offender
"pairs" to be relatives. This is not news, as any police officer will
tell you that the most dangerous calls to answer are those reported
as a family quarrel. Boudouris in a forty-two-year study of homicide cases in Detroit found that 30 percent of the pairs were related.[2] Voss and Hepburn found that one out of every two of the

1965 victims in Chicago were related to their offenders.[3] Willie,[4] Fields and Field,[5] and Wolfgang[6] found similarly high family related incidence in their studies of murders committed in the United States. Straus, in his national study, reported that 1.8 million couples experience *spouse abuse* annually.[7] He stated, "The predominant position of the family as a setting for violence seems to apply to every form of physical violence from slaps to torture and murder. In fact, some form of physical violence between family members is so likely to occur at some point in the life cycle that it can be said to be almost universal."

There is considerable disagreement as to whether or not husbands are as frequently abused by their wives as wives are by their husbands. Steinmetz and Fields-Kirchner debate this issue well.[8] Certainly, women appear more frequently at refuges/shelters, emergency rooms, and in divorce courts, complaining of marital unhappiness and discord due to their husbands' aggressions. Husbands frequently note their bruises at alcohol treatment centers.

Kempe estimated that child abuse may occur as often as six times for every 1,000 births.[9] Zalba figured that between two hundred thousand and two hundred fifty thousand children annually need protective services in the United States.[10] Gil showed that the youngest of children—defenseless infants—are the most prone to severe abuse.[11] The National Center on Child Abuse and Neglect (NCCAN) estimates that one million children are mutilated by their parents each year. Of these children, one hundred thousand to two hundred thousand are physically abused, sixty thousand to one hundred thousand are sexually abused, and approximately seven hundred thousand are neglected. According to the 1978 American Humane Association Clearinghouse statistics, 37.6 percent of those involved 10-18-year-olds: 66 percent were neglect cases and 33 percent were abuse cases.[12] Unlike their younger sibs, adolescents can run away, speak out, and even protect themselves. Nevertheless, adolescent abuse remains prevalent throughout the statistical charts. Child sexual abuse is thought to primarily concern adolescents; the most common form being father/stepfather-daughter incest. Incestuous relationships usually begin with sexual advances while the daughter is in her latency years and progresses to intercourse when the daughter matures. Adolescent victims of abuse and neglect may run away to escape their predicament. Because running away from home is a status offense in every state, these attempts by the adolescents to escape maltreatment at home may ultimately result in juvenile court involvement.

Rivaling the frequency of sexual abuse of the adolescent are incestuous relationships with the preschool child. This type of sexual abuse is extremely difficult to uncover. Generally the other parent calls for help, or the information is divulged as part of the unfolding of another family stress.

Extreme violence perpetrated by children is the exception rather than the rule. However, when it does occur it is usually symptomatic of deteriorating parent-child relationships. Parents are usually the victims of child murderers, and often these killings reciprocate parental brutality to each other or the child.[13] But children often abuse each other. Gelles found that actual or threatened sibling violence was "a way of life."[14] Rarely does this violence lead to death, but, as Adelson showed, the preschool child is quite capable of homicidal rage when his position in the family is threatened.[15]

Older adult children, themselves often parents, increasingly resort to physical or emotional abuse of their parents—"granny bashing." Causes may be frustration due to the reversal of dependency roles, economic restraints, and the lessening of the elders' power in family decision making. The aggression may even sometimes be an opportunity to "get even" for years of family violence. Grandmothers, in particular, find themselves victimized too often by their adult children.

WHY FAMILY VIOLENCE NOW?

Family violence has been known, accepted, tolerated, and regulated since the recording of the written word. Suddenly, it has emerged as a social problem discovery of major proportions. Why now? What's new? Why is the media so concerned now? Why the rise in anti-family violence organizations and treatment centers? Why is there new legislation concerning violence in families?

"What's new and why now" may be answered by looking at the challenge facing the family concept and structure. Increasingly, during the end of the nineteenth century and throughout the twentieth century, society has become accustomed to viewing the family as independent, nuclear, and increasingly separate from the extended family such as grandparents, cousins, etc. Suddenly, the nuclear family construct is being challenged, as exhibited by rising divorce rates and alternate family forms. The family state is in flux. The tension resulting from this flux has led to scrutinization of the family's successes ... and failures. A universal search for the means to strengthen the family from within and without can be seen in many forms. All of these efforts have been undertaken to buttress the nuclear family's standing versus societal pressures for disintegration and anomie.

A second answer to the "what's new, why now" question centers around the mounting trend in western civilization towards sexual equality, particularly in marriage and at work. A slowly growing movement, inaugurated perhaps by the eloquent work of John Stuart Mill (1869), has been developing that is primarily aimed at enhancing women's and children's rights in juxtaposition to the needs of capitalism and growing nations.[16] Equal rights means equal rights within a family structure. The patriarchal dominance is being challenged.

Detailed histories of various family violence forms through the centuries can be found.[17] These histories tend to focus upon the issues of equality of the sexes, upon religious persecution, matriarchal versus patriarchal societies, or upon children as property and the need for laborers. Family violence or violence within the families is rarely addressed per se. Instead, child abuse, spouse abuse, and the like are dealt with separately, as if other forms of family violence did not exist. Not only are they rarely considered together, but individual movement/issue proponents find themselves as antagonists. Looking back over the last century, one finds a "see-saw" struggle between the championing of the rights of children (child abuse, child labor, and child advocacy laws) and of the rights of women (wife abuse, woman suffrage, and equal pay laws) for the attention and financial support of the people. *(Heaven help those on the other side of the fence who are hoping to stop abuse of the elderly.)*

In today's world of family violence, evidence of the same struggle exists. For example, "domestic violence" has become the

umbrella term for spouse abuse, particularly wife battering. In no
way does the name change suggest that the children's rights-wom-
en's rights issue and struggle for the power within the "same pie"
is diminished. Often found within these groups are those who advocate rescuing the victim and punishing, counseling, or separating
the abuser, versus those who place blame for the abuse on the
interaction and contributing roles of all members of the family in
the identified abuse. Still a third group has recently expanded to
unite all forms of violence among the family in to one "systems
approach." Advocates for the systems approach argue that the
"blame" should be spread among the entire family system, spot-
lighting all parties. Family violence, no matter what form, is still
family violence, and one form of family violence is likely to re-
place or be found concomitant to another form of family violence.

THE FAMILY SYSTEMS ORIENTATION
TO FAMILY VIOLENCE

Thus, with the emergence for the first time of an integrated
approach, which signals the development of a singular treatment
policy and theory to address and unite all forms of violence in
families, there becomes a third reason for "Why now?"
The systems approach to family violence assumes that:
1. violence affects *every* member of the family,
2. violence against one member is reflected to, present, or
   impending with other family members,
3. violence is tolerated with every family member having a
   relationship regarding it,
4. violence against any family member will stop when the
   family unit agrees to disallow it,
5. a single member of the family can change the family system, and thereby change the climate that permits violence
   in the family, and
6. when one member of the family changes his/her role regarding the violent acts, all other members will change/ad-
   just their roles accordingly.
The systems approach assumes that the inappropriate violent
behavior serves a purpose in helping to maintain the family.

Family systems protagonists believe that taking this approach will lead not only to utilizing scarce resources to better aid such families, but also will lead to the development of new resources. Advocating for one form of family violence against or in competition with another, family systems proponents believe, leads to poorer use of scarce resources and to lesser, not greater, development of new resources.

RELATED FACTORS TO THE FAMILY VIOLENCE SYSTEM

Violence and extreme aggression in the family is a *coping/problem-solving mechanism*. Initially it works, it resolves conflicts, it relieves stress, and it does so by reestablishing the "steady state." The aggressor reestablishes his/her authority, but the problem at hand will reemerge. There must be an immediate reactive solution to affecting change. Any attempt to stop family violence must be as effective as the violent act (a difficult challenge for the counselor). One must point out that *conflict is inevitable* in all families, but aggression should not be the solution.

How can family members, particularly adults, tolerate being a part of the abuse syndrome? There are many answers to this question. In the first place, *abusive people are not abusive all the time*, and *victims are not victims all the time*. Thus, one hesitates to leave a secure relationship that may seem good, or at least peaceful, the vast majority of the time. In the second place, aggression and its family violence forms are *learned behaviors*, passed down through the generations, culturally ingrained. Children learn love . . . and violence are synonymous, not being able to separate out the parent who strikes from the one who loves. In the third place, family violence may even meet the *basic human need for touching*, if that's the extent of touching in a family. Fourth, individuals and society have *different thresholds* of violence, e.g. we cannot agree on the limits of spanking, nor the limits of violence on television. Fifth, the stresses of society's sexual stereotyping and economic fluctuations impinge on the family most vividly within the privacy of the family home where the turmoil remains hidden from public scorn under the privilege and rights of the *sanctity of the universal home*. Finally, sixth, family violence permits *avoidance of family/marital conflict*. The abuser, in promulgating inappropriate behavior, actually supports family maintenance for the family in reaction to the aggression and will either coalesce, avoiding the trouble issue, or initiate new behaviors to avoid further aggression. That is, the spouse abuser may actually stop an impending divorce, or the child abuser may be keeping the mother around to prevent further abuse.

One cannot underestimate the association of the impact that alcohol (and other drugs) has upon the presence and extent of violence in the family. Alcohol's role is weaved in or inferred to throughout this book (and especially in the designated alcohol and family violence chapters). Whether actually dulling one's senses, or providing an excuse for an inexcusable act, the presence of alcohol from moderate to excessive levels within family member's biosystems tends to increase the likelihood and frequency of aggression among a significant number of individuals.

THE ACTORS/ROLES IN THE ABUSING FAMILY SYSTEM

The "triangular relationship" is a theoretical construct gaining wide acceptance among family system believers. The triangle-based theories of interpersonal relationships assume that it takes three people to stabilize an interpersonal relationship. These relationships become pathological when they rigidify and stop growth. The family violence pathological triangle may be viewed as three individuals or subsets of the system locked into three roles: the abuser (perpetuator, aggressor), the victim (helpless, passive), and the rescuer ("goody two-shoes"). At any given time, a family member may be stuck in one of these roles, but over time individuals may exchange roles.[18]

All abusers tend to have the following characteristics in common:

1. Their behavior was learned from the family of origin.
2. They project blame for the event on the victim.
3. They are extremely possessive and jealous of the victim.
4. They have inappropriate expectations of the victim ("perfect wife," adult behavior for a child . . . .)
5. They cannot remember details surrounding the assault or

even the assault itself (blackout).

The victims, also, seem to share some commonalities:

1. They tend to be socially isolated.
2. They internalize blame, feel shame and guilt, agreeing with the abuser, "I must be bad to have deserved this."
3. Despite the abuse, the victim remains very loyal.
4. By taking a helplessness role, the victim often learns to manipulate and control the enmeshed two others.

Finally, the rescuers all too often share good intentions, and yet they have a strong need to control others, and thus "goodness and need" leads to the pathological "triangulation," wherein the rescuer finds him/herself caught in a collusion pairing with the abuser or the victim against the other. Inevitably, the rescuer then becomes the next victim.

In families, the pathological triangle serves to create collusions across generational boundaries. Thus, the child may share a parental role, and a parent may become the child. Roles and responsibilities often become blurred and expectations confused.

INTERVENTION

For family violence to decrease and eventually disappear as a social problem, society first must no longer tolerate its existence. Societal attitudes must change away from prejudice towards the abusers and victims to placing the blame on the family system. The media must not be permitted to support family violence. A community sense must be developed, working against family isolationism. Family safety zones, shelters, and family negotiating centers must be created and supported. These family buffer zones must be established to support the maintenance of the family and not its desensitization.

Therapists, counselors, and police must not allow themselves to be placed in the rescuer role of the pathological triangle. This can be accomplished by: (1) helping each individual member achieve his/her own goals and strengthen their individual powers in negotiations with the family at large, and (2) reinforcing separation of parent-child responsibilities.[19] This can be accomplished by competent interagency case management and by maintaining a focus on the family process as a whole, thereby helping the family get

The Many Faces of Family Violence

on with the business of growing and maturing.

The following chapters delve with much greater detail into the dynamics of a general family systems framework, including theoretical constructs, policy effects, and social and clinical interventions suggested herein.

REFERENCES

1. Freeman, M. *Violence in the Home.* London: Saxon House, 1979.
2. Boudouris, J. "Homicide and the Family." *Journal of Marriage and the Family*, Vol. 33, pp. 667-677. 1971.
3. Voss, H., and Hepburn, J. "Patterns in Criminal Homicide in Chicago." *Journal of Criminal Law Criminology*, Police Science, Vol. 59, No. 4, pp. 499-508, 1968.
4. Willie, W. "Citizens Who Commit Homicides." *Revista Interamericana De Psicologia* (Buenos Aires) Vol. 4, No. 2, pp. 131-144. 1973.
5. Fields, M., and Field, H. "Marital Violence and the Criminal Process: Neither Justice Nor Peace." *Social Services Review*, 1973, Vol. 47, pp. 221-240.
6. Wolfgang, M.E. *Patterns in Criminal Homicide.* New York: John Wiley and Sons, 1958.
7. Straus, M., Gelles, R., and Steinmetz, S. *Violence in the American Family-Behind Closed Doors.* Garden City, New York: Anchor Press/Doubleday, 1980.
8. Fields, M., and Kirchner, R. "Battered Women Are Still in Need: A Reply to Steinmetz." *Victimology: An International Journal*, Vol. 3, Nos. 1-2, pp. 216-226, 1978. Steinmetz Reply, pp. 222-224.
9. Kempe, C.H. et al. "The Battered Child Syndrome." *Journal of the American Medical Association*, Vol. 181, p. 17, 1962.
10. Zalba, S.R. "The Abused Child II: A Typology for Classification and Treatment." *Social Work*, Vol. 12, No. 1, pp. 70-79, Jan., 1967.
11. Gil, D. *Violence Against Children.* Cambridge: Harvard University Press, 1970.
12. American Humane Association. *National Analysis of Official Child Neglect and Abuse Reporting.* Denver: American Humane Association, 1978.
13. Steinmetz, S. *The Cycle of Violence*, New York: Praeger, 1977.
14. Gelles, R. *The Violent Home.* Beverly Hills: Sage Publications, 1974.
15. Adelson, L. "The Battering Child." *Journal of the American Medical Association.* No. 222, pp. 159-161, 1972.
16. Mill, J.S. *The Subjection of Women*, New York: D. Appleton and Company, 1869.
17. Freeman, M. op. cit. pp. 1-8.
18. Flanzer, J.P. "The Vicious Circle of Alcoholism and Family Violence." *Alcoholism*, pp. 30-32, Jan.-Feb., 1981.

19. Flanzer, J.P. "Family Focused Management: Treatment of Choice for Deviant and Dependent Families." *International Journal of Family Counseling*, Vol. 6, No. 2, New York, 1978, pp. 25-31.

Chapter 2

CHARACTERISTICS OF FAMILY VIOLENCE

Barbara Star

Most people enter the realm of family violence research by the side door, not confronting the total phenomenon, but only one segment of it. In 1975, I began to conduct formal research with battered women. In addition to questionnaires and personality tests, I conducted face-to-face interviews with the women. Almost immediately it became apparent that there were variations in both the quality and type of abuse that the women reported. Most cases illustrated what I call *confined abuse,* i.e. where one family member was consistently the target of the assault. Because the setting in which I conducted the research was a shelter for battered women, it was usually the woman who was the sole target. However, in some cases, I found that the abuse was *global,* i.e. it extended to one, two, or even all family members. In some instances, the abuse was *multiple;* the assaults were sexual as well as physical.

I encountered a situation that was both global and multiple when I was involved as an expert witness in a court case that dealt with a woman who had killed her husband. The case had twice previously ended in hung juries. The district attorney, who might have offered to plea bargain, decided to prosecute a third time, because he had heard from a witness that the defendant was withholding information. It turned out that information had indeed been withheld, but not quite what the prosecuting attorney had anticipated.

The defendant had been married fourteen years and during most of that time she had experienced some form of physical abuse from her husband. His favorite technique was to grab her by the hair and smash her face against the wall, or a table, or the steering wheel of the car, which ever happened to be handy. He also punched and kicked her. The two oldest children had also been physically abused. This information was known and had been described in the prior trials. What had been suppressed was not a plot to kill the husband, as the prosecuting attorney had suspected, but two pieces of information that embarrassed and humiliated the family members. One piece of information was provided in the testimony of the oldest daughter. The twelve-year-old girl testified that, in addition to hitting her, the father had also begun sexual contact with her during that past year. The second piece of information came from the defendant who, amidst loud, racking sobs, let the full story come spilling out. The thing she had never told anyone was that several times her husband had tried to force her to participate in aberrant sexual acts and that one of those acts included an attempt to have her couple with an animal.

Characteristics of Abuse

If nothing else, this story illustrates what I have found to be the hallmark of family violence: violence that goes unchecked, spreads. Although some violence is never perpetrated on more than one family member, there is no way to guarantee that, once initiated, violence will remain focused on one target. Clinical experience suggests that once violence begins, it becomes more difficult for the abuser to limit its use.

However, this case included several other findings that are frequently associated with family violence and that I consider to be characteristic of abusive situations. One is that violent behavior accelerates over time. Violence increases in severity and in frequency. The shove becomes a slap, the slap becomes a punch, and the punch results in hospitalization. Another characteristic is that there is no need for prolonged arguments, no need for haranguing or hassling, to produce a violent encounter.

Each incident requires less provocation to trigger a physical assault. Sometimes people are just looking for an excuse to pick a fight, looking for a way to let loose with a torrent of physical blows. A third characteristic is that gradually assaulters must substitute external control for internal control. The ego mechanisms that help us test reality, understand the consequences of our behavior, and inhibit destructive behavior are weakened over time. Consequently, assaulters become more and more dependent on external control to stop their assaultive behavior. It may require intervention from the police or a neighbor or that a family member physically restrains the abuser. Another finding is that emotional abuse both precedes and accompanies the physical violence. There are put-downs and swearing. People are made to feel worthless, no good, inept, inconsequential, insignificant, and less than human. The emotional abuse stays with that person far longer than most of the physical injuries. Another general finding is that the use of alcohol increases the risk of injury. Alcohol may not be involved in every incident or may not even be consumed in large quantities, but, because it is a disinhibitor, the use of alcohol always increases the risk that serious injury will occur. The final characteristic of family violence is the self-propelling quality of the abusive action. Once the physical behavior is initiated it seems to take on a life of its own. I spoke with a man who said, "You know, I remember that I'd start hitting her and saying to myself, 'What are you doing, man? This is bad. You're hurting this person.' But I couldn't stop the arm. I just kept hitting and hitting." So, it is not that people don't know it is wrong, it is just that they are unable to stop.

Characteristics of Assaulters and Victims

Assaulters

I have been working very hard to overcome what I feel is a fragmented approach to family violence. We study bits and pieces of violent behavior as though they are unrelated. We study the way parents treat their children, the way adults treat their elderly parents, and the way husbands and wives deal with each other. I try to look for the commonalities in behavior that underlie the various forms of abuse. I realize there are differences, and they are important to identify and understand, but, I want to call to your attention the traits common to assaulters because too often they are overlooked. For example, violence occurs in the family of origin among assaulters much more often than among nonassaulters. It is not even a matter of dispute anymore because it has been cited repeatedly in studies and case histories. The mere witnessing or experiencing of abuse does not necessarily lead to later violence. There are many factors associated with subsequent violence. A study by McCord and Howard, in 1961[1], compared a total of 174 boys who were placed in one of three categories: overtly aggressive, meaning that they engage in fist fights and bullying behavior almost all of the time; assertive with sporadic hostility, meaning they were involved in fights sometimes; and nonaggressive, those boys who had very few outbursts of anger or rage. The researchers found several factors that foster aggression in children. Direct parental attacks toward the child, such as punitive discipline, frequent use of threats, and constant unfavorable comments about the child, were of prime importance. However, many other factors were associated with later violence that did not involve physical violence as a referent in the child rearing area. The researchers discovered that the families of the overtly aggressive boys tended to show intense conflict between the parents: one parent held the other parent in very low esteem and was quite verbal in making that clear or the parents were dissatisfied with the roles they held — as though their lives were empty and meaningless. They found that parents of the aggressive children frequently disagreed on the methods of childrearing, some of them preferring very rigid disciplinary techniques and others of them saying, "Leave the kids alone and let them grow." Consequently, parental discipline was inconsistent: the severity of punishment did not always match the magnitude of the child's act. They also found that the parents of the aggressive children were not overtly affectionate to one another. Just as we learn to be violent by watching people engage in violent actions, we learn to be loving by watching people engage in loving actions. That means hugging, kissing, and touching in nonviolent ways. There was no role model for that kind of behavior within the families of aggressive children.

In addition to being raised in families characterized by abuse, parental disagreements about child rearing, and lack of affection, my research revealed several other traits characteristic of assaulter behavior. I found that assaulters externalize blame. They place responsibility for their actions outside of themselves. They search for guilt-reducing rationalizations such as blaming the victim — "It's all your fault. You made me get mad at you," — someone or something else — the devil made me do it, "It wasn't my fault, it was the alcohol talking."

Another common characteristic among assaulters is their attempt to displace their anger. They shift anger that is meant for authority figures, like a boss or teacher, on to a family member where there are fewer chances for serious reprisals of their behavior. They also carry with them anger and resentment meant for parents or caretakers and displace these feelings inappropriately on to current family members, usually spouses or children. For instance, I knew a boy who had learned to hate weekends when he was growing up because weekends meant that his father would be coming home drunk. When this happened, the father beat the daylights out of everybody around him. The boy was beaten, the mother was beaten, the other children in the family were beaten. All through childhood the boy wanted to get back at his father. He hated to watch his mother being beaten, but he realized that he was too young and too small to try to intervene without really getting hurt in return. During all of his growing up days, while other children were playing and having a good time, he was nurturing his resentment. The thought that kept him going day after day was, "Wait 'til I get big enough. He's never going to hurt anybody ever again." Sure enough, when he reached adolescence he was able to do something about it. The next time his father hit the mother, the boy grabbed the man, punched him, knocked him to the ground and was going to smash him when the mother began pulling him away shouting, "Stop, stop. Don't hurt your father!" Imagine how he felt after all those years of building up to this very event — he was finally going to be the protector, finally going to do something about the abuse — and then his mother stops him. He could not understand it. The disillusionment was incredible. Had she really liked getting beaten all those years? Why hadn't she fought back? Why hadn't she protected the children? All of those thoughts became wrapped up with women in general. When he married he began hitting his wife. He says, "I don't understand why I do it. She is really a good person and doesn't deserve that kind of treatment." It is easy to understand his behavior in light of his early experiences with violence and disillusionment. He was taking out on his wife the anger he felt toward his parents.

Assaulters are highly possessive of their victims. They view their victims as their own property to do with as they please. Possessiveness brings with it the right to exert control. In many cases, that control is reflected in extreme jealousy. Almost invariably, it is reflected in the belief that they have the right to tell their victims what they want and the victim must comply. "Don't argue with me," says the irate parent. "You do what I tell you or else." One abusive parent complained to the judge that his two-year-old son was a willful child who needed stern discipline. The young boy was beaten because he did not speak in a tone that the parent felt conveyed the proper respect. For several hours the boy was made to say, "Please" and "Thank you" to the parent. Each time he was beaten and told, "That's still not right. Do it again."

Assaulters typically hold distorted perceptions of their victims that produce major role confusions. The assaulters expect their victims to meet a wide range of deep and unfulfilled needs. Often the assaulters expect the victims to perform functions that are inappropriate either to the status or the age of the victim. The outburst of rage results when the victims cannot, or will not, adequately meet those expectations.

Victims

Victims also display certain identifiable traits. Victims often were raised in emotionally restrictive home environments in which were encouraged to be passive, not to take action on their own behalf, and certainly not to show strong emotions. A second characteristic is that victims are socially isolated.

That means they have little or no opportunity for feedback from outside sources that can modify the violent situation. It also means that victims are unable to test the severity of the abuse, the reason for the abuse, or ways to deal with the abuse. For all they know, violence occurs in every family. A very important and almost universal trait is that victims internalize the blame for the abuse that they receive. They assume responsibility for the violent situation. They believe that they "cause" the assaults because of something they did, such as argue with the assaulter, or because they failed to perform an assigned task, or because somehow they did not live up to the expectation set by the assaulter. Their willingness to carry the burden of guilt in the family reduces the assaulters' need to accept responsibility for their own behavior.

A fourth trait is compliance. People who resort to physical violence are successful, in part, because their victims cooperate and rarely fight back. Although from the victim's viewpoint compliance is seen as a survival mechanism, assaulters perceive compliance as agreement and, as such, it provides the tacit approval necessary for continued acts of violence. There is one other factor that I find present among victims, loyalty. It is astonishing how often victims defend and attempt to rationalize the assaulter's violent behavior. Something in family relationships prompts the need to minimize the cruelty inherent in abusive acts. "I know he only acted that way because he was under pressure," contend some spouses. Abused children placed in foster care often express the desire to return to the abusive family unit. Perhaps the loyalty reflects a sense of hope that the situation will change or perhaps it is because assaulters are not always violent. Sometimes they are loving and kind. Mostly, the loyalty reflects a deep sense of ambivalence that we hold towards people who have meaning to us. We want their approval. It is a way to rationalize our own reluctance to let go of the relationship.

Reactions to Violence

The three most common reactions to violence are depression, fear, and impaired trust. The depression occurs when people feel they cannot take effective action to change their lives. "Sometimes I think I must be a ghost, and no one can hear me," said a middle-aged abused wife. "I talk, but no one seems to listen." Eventually they give up. They internalize all of that anger and turn it into a sense of futility and despair. Even among children, withdrawal is evident. Galdston observed a profound apathy among many of the physically abused children he examined in a Boston hospital.[3] To him they resembled cases of "shell-shock" that have been seen in adults. Initially, the children were motionless, passive, and unresponsive to external stimuli. It required continuous efforts by nursing personnel to restore connectedness and interaction with the environment.

Martin Symonds, a psychologist, developed a concept he called "frozen fright," which is sometimes associated with extreme fear-producing situations. Even though he applies the concept to people who have been assaulted by strangers, I think that it applies to family violence as well. He found that people who had been held in fearful situations for a long time, such as in a kidnapping, behaved, on the surface, in ways that made them seem to have participated in their own suffering by cooperating with the assaulters. When questioned later on, he found that the level of their fear was so deep that these people had submerged the fear and performed superficial acts that made their behavior look like collaboration when, in fact, it was not. In reality, it was a deeply ingrained sense of terror, a terror so overwhelming that the victims felt hopeless about escaping and believed their survival depended on their ability to appease the assaulter. I am certain that family members, who live with the constant threat of physical violence, submerge their fears in a similar way. They seem to be collaborating in their own victimization, but their compliance may be the only way for them to survive.

The third reaction is impaired trust, which may be the most devastating consequence of abuse. People wonder not only about what will happen to them in other relationships that they enter, whether they can risk the vulnerability of caring, but also whether they even have anything to offer in those relationships. They have withheld love for so long, they have withheld themselves for so long, that they honestly do not know if they have anything of value to offer someone else.

Treatment

In general, family violence can be dealt with by differentiation, reeducation, and restructuring. When making a determination of treatment needs, the first step is to differentiate. Family violence should be differentiated on the basis of frequency, severity, target, and when it began. Your techniques will be modified by each of those factors. For example, a person who is beaten daily might require immediate placement in a foster home or shelter whereas a person who suffers a beating once a year might not be in the same state of crisis. Reeducation is called for because frequently violent behaviors occur in conjunction with a lack of knowledge about the right, appropriate, or best ways to act in certain situations. It is necessary to consider such things as what are appropriate child rearing actions, the appropriate level of assertiveness, realistic appraisals of personal skills, and realistic expectations of others' behavior. The last area has to do with restructuring, that is, changing the environment so that the same conditions are not present over again. For example, if isolation is a problem, then develop a support network for the person or the family. I happen to believe that sometimes separation is very important because it allows people to leave the immediate embroiling situation and think things through. So the need for shelters and quiet environments may be as essential for assaulters as for the victims of abuse.

No matter what treatment strategies we finally develop, please remember that violence can kill. So, whatever else you do, your first priority is for the physical safety of the family members.

BIBLIOGRAPHY

Elbow, M.: Theoretical considerations of violent marriages. *Social Casework, 58:*515-526, 1977.
Gladston, R.: Observations on children who have been physically abused and their parents. *American Journal of Psychiatry, 122:*440-443, 1965.
Jameson, P. and Schellenbach, C.: Sociological and psychological factors of male and female perpetrators of child abuse. *Child Abuse and Neglect, 1:*77-83, 1977.

McCord, W., McCord, J. and Howard, A.: Familial correlates of aggression in nondelinquent male children. *Journal of Abnormal and Social Psychology, 62:*79-93, 1961.

Meiselman, K.: *Incest.* San Francisco, Jossey Bass, 1978.

Rathbone-McCuan, E.: Elderly victims of family violence and neglect. *Social Casework, 60:*30-38, 1979.

Star, B.: Patterns in family violence. *Social Casework, 61:*339-346, 1980.

Symonds, M.: Victims of violence: Psychological effects and aftereffects. *American Journal of Psychoanalysis, 35:*19-26, 1975.

Chapter 3

LONG-TERM TREATMENT ISSUES WITH BATTERED WOMEN

Kathryn Conroy

Little has been written regarding the long-term treatment issues involved in working with battered women. After the immediate crisis is over and after a decision has been made whether to stay in the relationship or not, how then does the victim and the counselor/therapist proceed with the course of treatment?

To answer this question it is necessary to address the core of the issue: ambivalence. At the same time, we must look at the coping responses that battered women use to stay in their relationships. We must also understand the interplay of psychological factors, learned socialization, and societal reinforcers (such as lack of resources and the dominant message of systems), which dictate that women remain married and in the home.

Women are taught from infancy to be ambivalent about themselves. In their article, "Ambivalence: The Socialization of Women," Bardwick and Douvan point out that for the young girl "ambivalence is clearly seen in the simultaneous enjoyment of one's feminine identity, qualities, goals and achievements and the perception of them as less important, meaningful, or satisfying than those of men."[1] From earliest childhood the female is socialized to not be aggressive, powerful, certain, or forceful—all

24

values applauded by society, but allowable only to men. To succeed in most of the valued arenas of daily living, on the job, in the marketplace, or in scholarship, it is essential to incorporate those attributes of power and certainty. But women have been forced to communicate these characteristics in a covert manner, thus valuing the ability to be aggressive, clear, and powerful because of what these behaviors can achieve, but feeling badly about themselves for having employed them.

This ambivalence is reinforced in the family where wives, because of their isolated, devalued position, are cast in potential victim roles. In a society where women are going to work in waged jobs in greater numbers than ever before, it is not usual for the woman to do so out of professional desire or because her capacity to earn is greater than her husband's. Rather, her employment is subject to her husband's approval, and he views it as merely supplemental to his income. Her work outside the home is valued less than her husband's and her work in the home is not valued at all since it is something she is "supposed to do."

Ambivalence regarding violence in relationships is also rooted in the family. As Murray Straus has pointed out, there is an early linking for the child between violence and caring.[2] The parent who sees the child reaching for the pot of boiling water pulls the child away and slaps his/her hand, because they care enough to teach a life-sustaining lesson. Parents slap or spank often because they care and verbally say so while hitting their child. For most people, the first person to be violent towards them, to intentionally physically hurt them, was a parent. This right of the parents to hurt the child because they care is dramatically and symbolically passed on in marriage as the father of the bride walks her down the aisle and hands her over to the groom. Until recent years the legal *right* of husbands to corporally discipline their wives was not challenged.

In the face of this analysis what are the coping responses used by battered women? In her article, "Violent Families: Coping Responses of Abused Wives," Jane Pfouts describes four.[3] She lists the typology of battered women, which may be viewed as a continuum, and is constructed as follows:

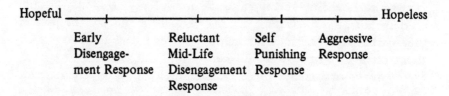

Hopeful ————————————————————————————— Hopeless

| Early Disengage- ment Response | Reluctant Mid-Life Disengagement Response | Self Punishing Response | Aggressive Response |

Briefly, according to Pfouts, the woman in the "Early Disengagement Response" sees alternatives for herself, has resources, and when beaten either leaves the relationship or threatens to leave in such a way that her husband knows she can and will. The "Self-Punishing Response" is the woman who blames herself for being in the violent marriage. Seeing no resources for help reaffirms her belief that she is at fault. The "Reluctant Mid-Life Disengagement Response" is the woman who blames herself for the violent marriage, but reluctantly decides to leave it, not because she believes she should not be beaten, but because the violence has become so great that she is either afraid for herself or for her children. The "Aggressive Response" is the woman who meets violence with violence. The resulting "peace" resembles the world's peace where no one fights because everyone is assured of the others capacity to retaliate. Pfout's sample consisted of only thirty-five cases, many of which fall into the "Reluctant" and "Self-Punishing" categories. It is a tribute to her perceptive ability that we have seen her broad topology hold true with hundreds of clients.

The work of the long-term therapist is to help the woman move to a point on the continuum between "early" and "reluctant" disengagement responses, where an "I" statement is possible. For a battered woman the "I" statement consists of her ownership of the belief that no one, specifically she, deserves to be beaten or should be beaten. She comes to recognize her ambivalence in changing the battering situation, while understanding how social systems have not helped her in the past and have even contributed to her staying. She comes to realize that she is not the cause or the reason for the battering, but that she is solely responsible for staying in the relationship or leaving it and that viable help is real. Until a battered woman gets to this "I" position and can own these statements, she will be unresolved in permanently changing her situation.

The elements of "Hopeful" and "Hopeless" on the continuum are a contribution of Susan Schechter.[4] Perhaps they most clarify the dilemma of ambivalence for women. Girls/Women are socialized to believe that marriage is desirable and, in some groups, mandatory. Women are also socialized to believe that they are responsible for holding the marriage together and for sacrificing in order to do so. In marriages, they continually hope things will get better, he will change, they can stop his drinking, reform his behavior, etc. For us, however, the "Hopeful" end of the continuum is the healthy "I" position that the woman takes regarding her violent marriage. It is hopeful because she is taking charge of her life, resolving her historical and present ambivalence, learning to live despite internal dissonance, and making a decision, whether that decision is to leave the marriage, stay if he gets help, stay while she tries to get him help, etc. The "Hopeless" end of the continuum represents two types of battered women: (1) The "Self-Punishing Response" position, i.e. the women who believe it is their fault that the marriage is violent, who see no alternatives, and therefore no possibility for change; and (2) The "Aggressive Response" position, i.e. those women who believe that they are "taking care of business" because they have stemmed their husband's violence with their own. Until they see this uneasy "peace" as emotionally dysfunctional as the previous "war" they will not move to the hopeful end of the continuum.

Where does this leave the long-term therapist? The following material must be covered by the therapist whether the woman client comes to therapy because of the battering, or the fact of battering in a relationship comes up in the course of general therapy. Utilizing material presented by the battered woman, the therapist helps her cognitively review patterns of each battering event in the framework of the overlapping interplay of the psychological, societal, and socialization contributing factors.

Psychological factors are those deep-seated issues in a person's personality that require resolution or reconstruction in order for the client to make substantial movement in the other areas of her life. They are the factors with which therapists are the most familiar and comfortable. Socialization factors are those issues

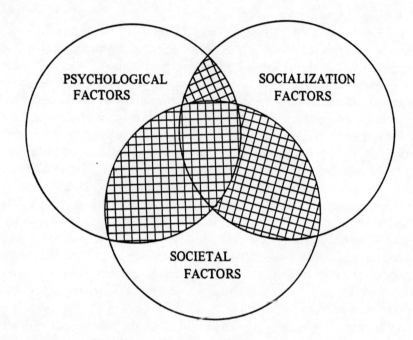

imposed by society as the "way things ought to be" (i.e. marriages "should" be happy or someone is at fault; women "should" hold families together).   Socialization factors are the realm of the "shoulds" and the beliefs that we pick up of "what we should be." Societal factors are anticipated, available, or the lack of community/environmental resources. The therapist's task is to evaluate with the client those factors that are most pressing in her staying in an unchanged situation. An evaluation of this kind is extremely necessary, since we know that (a) battering over time becomes more intense in each assault or the assault becomes more frequent; and (b) battering in a marriage does not change unless the battered woman leaves or the husband is motivated to change his behavior and goes for counseling.

An analysis of why the woman stays in an unchanged battering situation, and which factors impact on her staying, is possible by asking the woman client the following questions:

    a. What is *her* understanding of why she is being battered?
    b. What are her coping responses during and after a battering event?

    c. What is her rationale for staying in the battering relationship?

    d. What are her overall strengths and weaknesses as articulated by herself and by the therapist?

We are able to outline the course of treatment by asking these questions and by listening to and delving behind these answers.

What is her understanding of why she is being battered? Standard responses to this question include (but are in no way limited to): "He's jealous," "It only happens when he drinks," or "I'm not a good wife." Women will have some understanding of why this is happening to them. To not have a reason for "why" would be to view the world as capricious and out of control. All of our existence is based on the world being a "reasonable" place. Take what the woman gives as a reason and use it as such, exploring it carefully with her, for example, "I may be his excuse, but I have never been the reason," and go beyond it with her to enunciate the basis for the reason, listening primarily for psychological or socialization factors as causative.[5]

Do not be afraid to play back to her her own words in the interview, especially if she offers answers to this question in an offhand, superficial manner. The therapist with an understanding such as the one set forth here may be the first person who has seriously affirmed her reality; all others unconsciously, or not, try to avoid it. She may be so unused to someone willing to listen, who even suggests some action, that her personal distance from the incident(s) she is recounting may puzzle the therapist. As the question is asked, play back to her the answers, and look for the basic issue underlying her understanding of why the battering is happening.

It is important to understand the women's interpretation of the "event" of being battered. While Lenore Walker in her book *The Battered Woman* looks at the cycle of battering taking the course of days, weeks, or months, it may be more helpful to look at the individual incidents.[6] Each incident has its beginning, middle, and ending parallel to the three parts of the cycle Walker spreads over time. It has been helpful to have women recount these parts by looking at their most recent beating. Looking at almost any incident will yield much of the same information, however.

The "beginning" of the battering event may be verbal or non-verbal, and many batterers will verbally provide the excuse for their battering before the actual assault. This may take the form of berating the woman for not being a good wife, a good mother, or too silent, too talkative, etc. The woman must review with the therapist the content of the verbal exchange, the excuse preceding the actual assault. The information gleaned from the woman's perspective will provide certain insights for the therapist about the woman's own ambivalent issues. These issues may include "If I *were* a better wife, he wouldn't beat me"; "If I *didn't* look at other men *at all*, no matter how innocently"; etc. The therapist must show the woman that no matter how *she* has changed *her* behavior in the past the beatings still occurred. If the beginning of the battering event is nonverbal, if there is no attempt at providing an excuse or justification for the beating, then it would seem that the woman was subjected to the most arbitrary and capricious violence possible. Her world view would be skewed over time, with all reason in the relationship replaced by raw power.

The "middle" of the battering event is the assault itself. Documentation shows that battering of women centers on their breasts and abdomen (particularly feminine areas and body areas not likely to be seen), and that women who are battered in relationships are battered more severely and more often during pregnancy. In asking questions about the actual assault it is the therapist's agenda to ascertain the real level of danger. This may be difficult, as women will often minimize the actual damage done once they have some distance from it. Understandably so, for they are still living within the context of that danger. Soldiers who live under constant threat in time of war do much of the same distancing. While this distancing and minimizing of the danger is an adequate ego defense, it makes it more difficult for the therapist to ascertain the actual potential for harm.

The "end" of the battering event has implications for ambivalence also. If the husband apologizes, begs for forgiveness, promises never to let it happen again, he is reinforcing exactly what she wants to hear. He is telling her precisely what she wants to believe and what society tells her she *should* believe. If he does not apologize, he may verbally end the beating the way he verbally began it: he reinforces for her why he "had" to beat her and may even state that he hopes she has learned her lesson and will be better. The third alternative is that he says nothing, and the context of the beating hangs like a damning psychological/emotional cloud over the home.

The therapist must ask the woman, "What are your coping responses during and after a battering event?" In other words, "What do you do and think about while you are being battered and afterwards?" Many women will report that they felt quite distant from themselves while they were being battered. Like many victims of rape, they report that they felt as if they were standing apart from themselves and watching it happen. This is absolutely *normal* and, in fact, a good defense. Some will report a tremendous rage with feelings of aggression toward the batterer, but an inability to fight back because they were so overwhelmed. Some will answer, "I have to take it because I have no place to go." Her answers will give the therapist clues as to which factors have the most impact on her staying in an unchanging situation. Also important is to ask the question, "How did you feel and what did you do after the battering?" Lenore Walker makes the point that there can be a shift in power for some women after the battering event.[7] After the assault some men beg for forgiveness from their wives, thus placing them in the "powerful" position of forgiving or not. (The "powerful" position is only an illusion, because if she does not forgive she will surely be beaten until she does.) Some therapists will look to this period after the battering event for clues to secondary gains. While it is important for the therapist to look at all facets of the client's experience, it would be simplistic and erroneous to make the leap from the battered woman who feels no power in her life except when she has the "power" to forgive or not forgive her husband, "to" the battered woman "provokes" the battering in order to get to the position of power. The danger of this leap is to land up *blaming the victim*. Those women who report provoking the battering will also admit, when questioned, that they "knew they were going to get it" from his cues, so they provoked the event so that they could eke out some control as to the time and place. To live under the terrible pressure of knowing that one will be beaten, but not knowing when or how, is almost unimaginable and unbearable.

What is her rationale for staying? Reasons that women give have included "for the kids," "because no one in my family has ever been divorced," or "I love him". The reasons offered are far-ranging and have tremendous depth behind their face value. For example, "I love him" probably sums up the greatest ambivalence for women. Men who batter their wives are not ogres, they are not violent twenty-four hours a day, seven days a week. They probably have times of tenderness, warmth, and giving with their wives and children. If a woman decides to leave a battering man she is not only leaving behind the violent exchanges, but also the good times, the happy moments, and the fact that he may be a good provider. If she does not come to grips with the fact that she is losing these comforting aspects, as well as leaving behind the violent ones, then she will resolve her ambivalent feelings and will probably return later to an unchanged situation. She must also mourn the loss of her hope that the marriage will get better by itself or through her single actions. The therapist must help the woman mourn the loss of the person, the familiar situation, and the hope.

Often the reasons women give for staying are economic and are rooted in the lack of resources that society offers her. This analysis is accurate. If she leaves she will most likely suffer economically. Statistics show that men paying child support pay more infrequently, or not at all, as time goes on. It is very important then for the therapist to avoid discounting a woman's economic concerns about leaving a battering relationship. Rather, the therapist needs to view concerns as a societal factor to take into consideration. Issues such as "I stay for the kids" and "My family doesn't support divorce" are socialization factors and require work toward a long-term resolution. "I love him," if this means such dependency that the woman cannot conceive of being without him, may mean a psychological factor and require even more time toward resolution. Though a woman may decide to leave even though these issues are not resolved, this decision is usually based on immediate safety. The therapist's task is to interpret the rationale that had been used for staying and to resolve the issues of ambivalence around leaving.

What are her overall strengths and weaknesses? We often only sum up the weaknesses of battered women and overlook the reserve of strength that has enabled them to live in a threatening situation, often successfully raising her children, and providing for the functioning of the family. We don't look at the strengths she has used to remain sane in a highly disturbed situation. We must look at her socializing, psychological, and societal strengths. Helping her to mobilize these cognitive resources around the battering events and to take ownership of her actions toward resolution is critical.

Pragmatically, any therapist who is working with women is working with battered women. Battered women are statistically represented in every therapist's case load. Traditionally, battering has been avoided as an issue in the long-term therapeutic process. The information and validation of the existence of violence toward women in the home has not come from counselors/therapists. To affirm its existence would imply that something should be done about it, and up to now no one has known what to do, and resources have not existed. Therapists have also not been trained to work with violence or with victims. In most cities, and many communities, resources now exist, and a small but growing body of knowledge about battered women is now available. No longer can battered women be dismissed with the psychiatric jargon that calls them masochistic. The therapist's responsibility must include viewing the battered woman and her situation in a total framework that takes into account psychological factors, socialization factors, and societal resources.

REFERENCES

1. Gornick, V., and Moran, B. (Eds.): Women in sexist society. In *Ambivalence: The Socialization of Women*. Bardwick, J. and Douvan, E., New York: Basic Books, 1971, pp. 147-159.
2. Murray Straus in a lecture at the Mid-America Institute on Family Violence, Hot Springs, Arkansas, October, 1978.
3. Pfouts, J.H.: Violent Families: coping responses of abused wives. *Child Welfare*, (February): 101-111, 1978.
4. Susan Schechter, 1979: personal communication.
5. Martin, D., *Battered Wives*. San Francisco, Glide Publications, 1976, p. 3.
6. Walker, L.: *The Battered Woman*. New York, Harper and Row, 1979.
7. Walker, ibid.

Chapter 4

ALCOHOL AND FAMILY VIOLENCE

Jerry P. Flanzer

In the Western world, alcohol has long been associated with violence. Problem drinking and family violence is surely not new. Police officers will note their fear of having to enter a home to settle a violent marital fight complicated by alcohol. Three new developments (3 P's) have heightened and highlighted alcohol and family violence:

1. **Prevalence.** The staggering recent findings of the high prevalence of alcohol misuse among most forms of family related violence.
2. **Portrait.** The mounting clinical evidence showing the common "portrait" and/or behavioral styles of these two types of abusing families.
3. **Policy.** The legitimization of these problem practice arenas for the professional mainstream, greatly influenced by the concomitant concern on the national policy level.

CONCEPTS

Alcohol abuse incorporates a wide range of imbibing behaviors. Most of our known research centers around the alcoholic and frequent drinker, but there is little knowledge regarding the occasional and moderate drinker. Research regarding the effect of drinking alcohol on everyday, "normal" family life, surprisingly, is sparse and is of little consequence. It is easier to study the captive alcoholic patient and, perhaps, even the "driving while intoxicated" client than it is the general user of alcohol. Increasingly, the survey contained reports of the presence or contribution of alcohol to problems bringing clients through the intake services of medical or mental health clinics, protective services, and the courts. These surveys provide the data linking family violence to the aftermath of incidence drinking, weekend binges, and the like.[1,2]

"Family violence" is a misnomer. "Violence in families" is the preferred logo, for "family violence" infers that the cause lies within the family and that it is normal and expected. Violence in families includes physically, emotionally, or sexually harmful behavior through acts of commission or omission by one family member against another that may have its germination inside or outside of the family, hence allowing for the contribution of alcohol abuse to violence in the family, either as a family initiated problem or as an individual's problem affecting the family. The violence behavior within the family includes: family members physically abusing/severely emotionally neglecting another family member, child abuse, spouse abuse (including wife and husband beating and sexual abuse), abuse of the elderly, and sibling and teenage abuse. (The author acknowledges a wider definition of violence than in most "specific" literature. He takes a systems approach, noting that severe emotional neglect is every bit as damaging as physical abuse and even more likely to be associated with problem drinking.)

This intrafamily aggressive behavior is common, but by no means a necessary norm. Undoubtedly there are very few who have not been its victim, or its persecutor, or its rescuer.[3] Few parents have failed to spank their child harder than their original intent; few husband/wives have not been slapped at least once by a spouse in a moment of rage. These incidents are not considered pathological or dysfunctional unless they are repeated or become a part of a patterned behavior; unless the invisible and ill-defined line of "the harmful act(s) — the violence line" is crossed. When alcohol is involved, the chances of overstepping the violence line appear to be greatly increased.[4]

Most of us have been socialized to believe that alcohol is a disinhibitory agent, an aggression-release potion causing untold violence. In fact, the drunk is seen as sick and not responsible for his behavior, and indeed, abused spouse after spouse has bought into this belief system. Rarely is a marriage or family broken up due to the husband's/wife's drinking episodes. This is regardless as to how severe or bizarre the physical punishment is inflicted to the "loved" family member after drinking. In every case, another precipitating crisis must occur before relief or help is requested.[5]

Gelles notion of the "time-out" mechanisms adds the learned behavior dimension to this alcohol-aggressive idea.[6] One learns the behavioral comportments of drinking, takes "time-out" from the norms and demands of everyday life and aggresses — and after all, during this socially acceptable time-out he is not held responsible for his violent actions. Even the law cooperates, for the crime is often less when the violator has been drinking. Perhaps, then, individuals who wish to carry out a violent act become intoxicated in order to carry out the violent act and suffer less legal consequence.

An important and sad side effect of the popularizing of the alcoholic disease notion is that to have a drinking problem is no longer as shameful. Certainly it is less so than incest or wife beating. Thus, very often, the family wishing to avoid shameful stigmatization uses alcohol to disavow the deviance of violence in the family. As McGaghy first reported, aggressors often invoke the explanation that they were drunk and did not know what they were doing.[7] Then, the other family members are able to orchestrate an account that admits the occurrence of the deviant behavior, but maintains the definition of the family as normal, by focusing the blame on the alcohol that caused the abhorrent act.[6]

Unfortunately, alcohol abuse in itself by one of the family members increases the severity of the effects of the incident on the family and tends to further prevent the family from working through their problems.[8,4] Alcohol abuse, in many cases, is, of course, the initiating key to the never-ending abuse cycle. Often a primary conflict over drinking extends to other arguments concerning financial affairs and then to the interfamily relations of which sexual relation issues often predominate. Marital disputes are rehashed; dominance-submissive interaction issues surface.

The "ante" is raised until it is okay to "call in the chips" — an excuse for behavior unspeakable before the drinking precipitant normalizes the violence.

Let's look at some of the grim alcohol family violence associated facts, starting first with the children.

PREVALENCE

Alcoholism literature shows clearly that children of alcoholic parents are subject to a high risk of developing alcoholism in their adult years. Attention in recent years has increasingly focused on the alarmingly high incidence of emotional and behavioral disorders of this group.[9,10] Life in the home of an alcoholic parent can be chaotic, confusing, and unpredictable; it frequently involves parental neglect and even physical abuse of the children. Such children often have poor self-concepts, low frustration tolerance, poor school performance, and have numerous adjustment problems during the adolescent years. Twenty-five to fifty percent of all alcoholics have had an alcoholic parent or close relative.[11,12,13] The 25 million children of alcoholics are twice as likely to become alcoholic as the children of their nonalcoholic counterparts.[14,15] Besides the increased likelihood of birth defects due to pregnant alcoholic women, children of alcoholics are more likely to suffer from psychoses due to an increased likelihood of prolonged separation from parent(s) and inconsistent parental substitutes. As Hindman writes:

> Contributing to the emotional problems of such a child is the fact that the behavior of the alcoholic parent, and often that of the non-alcoholic spouse as well, tends to be erratic and inconsistent. The focus of family life is on the alcoholism; children are often ignored or neglected, disciplined inconsistently, and given few concrete limits and guidelines for behavior. In addition, the family is generally isolated from other members of the community. Because of the alcoholism problem there are few family outings or group activities at home. Friendships are avoided by both the non-alcoholic spouse and the children because they are ashamed of the presence of alcoholism in their family.[16]

Behling reported on the incidence of alcohol-related child abuse at one large clinic:

1. Fifty-seven percent of the abused/neglected children had at least one grandparent who was alcoholic or who abused alcohol.
2. Sixty-five percent of the suspected child abusers/neglectors were alcoholics or abused alcohol.
3. Eighty-eight percent of the previously abused parents were abused by an alcoholic or alcohol-abusing parent.
4. Eighty-four percent of the abused or neglected children had at least one parent who was alcoholic or abused alcohol.[17]

Miketic,[18] Grislain,[19] Popisil, Zarricki, and Turcin,[20] and Nau[21] came to similar conclusions of high incidence of alcoholism among child-abusing parents. Interestingly, Nau found that the alcoholic parent often committed the violent act when not intoxicated.[21] Spieker and Mousakitis found child abuse prevalent among alcohol abusers with severe and moderate problems and less likely among those with slight drinking problems.[2]

What about child neglect? Here the alcohol-child neglect literature is scarce. Note that the research citings are primarily concerned with alcoholics and alcoholism in their studies: lesser problem drinking or situational problem drinking effects are not separated out from chronic alcoholism.

Similarly, most of these findings refer to young children; for that matter, only scant attention in child abuse literature has been spent on the abused adolescent and that primarily related to incest. Ramee and Michau[22] and Virkkunen[23] do refer to cases relating alcoholic parents and incest. Chronic brutality and alcoholism are the two most frequently cited complaints of incestuous families.[24] Yet, child protective services report a growing significant case load of alcohol-related parents abusing and severely neglecting their children. Often when teenagers are involved, the child and parent are both abusing alcohol. Flanzer noted the association of drinking parents among the clinics specializing in child abuse and neglect case load. In a study reported with Sturkie, Flanzer noted that in a sample of sixty-five such abusive families, frequency did not associate with the prevalence of alcohol, but severity of the abuse to the child did. Although scant, similar findings can be found relating alcohol abuse and most other forms of violence in families. No literature is now available on alcohol abuse and abuse of the elderly or abuse by young children of their parents or siblings.

The question one might raise is, "Is there a difference between the mechanisms behind alcohol abuse and those of family violence?" For, indeed, the clinical portraits and causal explanations for each have been remarkably similar.

PORTRAIT

What does an alcohol-abusing family look like? What does an abusing family look like? Certainly, they cannot be lumped into one personality type, nor one interactional system mode, but generally the extent of the family pathology is related to the compulsivity of the abuse.

Some clinical trends, yet to be supported by hard research, have been noted in the literature. Family literature for compulsive alcohol abusers responds with a general family constellation that portrays the emotionally distant father coupled with an overly close mother-son relationship, marital disruptions, and a large number of early parental deaths. Hanson, Shanks, and Sheldon found alcoholic husbands to be less open and revealing about themselves and their feelings than their wives.[25] Rae and Drewery, in their study of marital patterns, found male alcoholic subjects to be more "feminine" than male controls, confused about their sociosexual roles, and more conflicted about needs for dependence and independence.[26] Gerard and Kornetsky found that the mothers of alcoholic adolescents were either excessively controlling and stern, or indulgent, nondisciplinary, and often seductive.[27] The father had either minimal or punitive roles. Schwartzman concurred: "The fathers were either authoritarian, but easily controlled by mother, or distant . . . more clearly secondary to the mother in terms of power."[28]

Over and over again the parental messages stress the worthlessness and unacceptability of the identified family violence abusing member. The abuser in this family constellation is always falling short, reenacting his own powerless, ineffective, guilt-ridden, and depressed family role assignment everywhere he goes in or out of therapy.

The high mortality-suicidal rate among alcoholics may be viewed in light of the preceding. The death wish, or instruction for the alcoholic to die, is often quite clearly expressed by the family. He is placed in the role of savior and martyr. His death is seen as a noble, cleansing sacrifice in which he is often a willing participant. According to Kempler and McKennon, the silent characteristics of families with an alcoholic parent who is then abusing adolescent children are:

· Poor relationships between parents and the same sex child;
· Severe marital dysfunction and overinvolvement between the adolescent and one parent;
· High incidence of current or past alcohol use in parents;
· Dysfunctional family communication and alienation;
· Symptoms in other children besides the identified patient.[29]

The family typically reacts to the abusing familial dysfunctioning, as do all organisms under stress and crisis, first by denial and avoidance; second by sporadic attempts or resolution with alternating periods of withdrawal and social isolation; and third, often after the "best" period for intervention, by breaking down in disorganization, chaos, and despair.[30,31]

Much has been written describing the "abusing" family, its roots and structure. Several themes are often repeated. First, there is the common belief that abusing parents were abused as children. This intergenerational idea has been suggested by Gunn[32] and reinforced by Smith, Henson, and Noble,[33] and Kempe,[34] all who note that children who are neglected tend to marry and conceive early and repeat the mistakes of their parents. Theoretically, then, the children of alcoholics/abusive parents are doomed. Alexander and Dibb pointed to deficient parenting skills leading to poor parental role models.[35] Spinetta and Rigler pointed out that child-abusing parents lack "hard" parenting facts.[36]

Abusing parents frequently lack appropriate knowledge of child rearing, and their attitudes, expectations, and child-rearing techniques set them apart from nonabusive parents. The abusive parents implement culturally accepted norms for rearing children, but with an exaggerated intensity and at an inappropriately early age. These parents often turn to children to meet their dependency needs and have low levels of empathy and a great emphasis on discipline and control.[37]   The results of a longitudinal study by DeLissovoy are relevant to this point of view.[38]   DeLissovoy studied marital adjustment in rural high-school-aged parents and found that a majority had unrealistic or erroneous ideas about developmental norms for young children. In addition, eighty percent of his subjects mentioned physical punishment as a method of control for children, and these themes have been found in abusive parents. Steele characterized abusive parents as (1) expecting unrealistically high levels of performance from their children; (2) viewing physical punishment as a necessary form of discipline; and (3) disregarding the helpless state, needs, and desires of the infants.[39]   Ignorance of developmental patterns in young children is viewed as a contributing factor to most accidents involving infants.[40]   As a result of a study of thirty case histories of young, emotionally disturbed mothers who were involved in child abuse, Burglass concluded a primary need in treatment was for abusive parents to obtain mothering skills.[41]

Straus argues that abusing parents learn this role from their own parents.[42]   Laury repeated this theme, suggesting that abusers may have been abused and, therefore, unwittingly imitate their parents.[43]   Several empirical studies appear to support this idea. Holter and Friedman studied eighteen families in which children had been abused.[44]   They found that the abusing parents had been frequently neglected and abused as children also. Two other studies that are related concerned infants characterized by "failure to thrive." Bullard studied fifty mothers of such infants and concluded that failure to thrive is caused by maternal deprivation.[45] Togut studied eighteen infants and their mothers and found that profound emotional and physical deprivation was a common characteristic in the mother's childhood experiences.[46]   This notion, that abuse may be part of the history of the abusing parent, is postulated by others as, at least, a contributing factor of misbehavior. In a study of eighty-five families, Johnson and Morse found that the majority of parents had suffered some degree of deprivation during their childhood.[47]

The first theme, "the intergenerational notion," is that persons who engage in violence tend to have been victims of violence (and this most often by their parents). We all have been victims of violence. Following David Bakan's reasoning:

Every time a child is punished by the use of violence or sees interfamily violence, he is being taught by his role models, or ego ideals,
that the use of violence is a proper mode of behavior. All he lacks is
the physical and social might . . . as soon as he gets it he acts as if it
were a 'right.' One of the greatest obstacles in dealing with an alcohol abuser, child abuser, spouse abuser, etc., is this feeling that the
actions were justified . . . as licensed and sanctioned by his original
parental figures.[48]

*A second theme is the belief that a common personality type
exists for abusing.* This once popular notion has fallen in every
category to research scrutiny.

*A third theme is the belief that severe familial crisis leads to
regression and generational breakdowns.* Jackson, in her alcoholism studies, has suggested that when a family is subjected to a continuing series of crises or accumulating stress, abuse may occur as
an indication of failure of the family members in coping with
their problems.[49]   This stress overload leads to an inability to
cope.   Several child abuse studies   confirm Jackson's findings
(*see* Callaghan and Fotheringham[50] and Elmer[51]). In a study of
forty-five cases of failure to thrive, Evans found that one group of
child-abusing mothers perceived the abused child as one more
crisis in a life of chronic crises.[52] Hecht[53] and Seldin[54] worry
about the complex pattern of behaviors learned through role
modeling of parents, such as moral judgment, that Burke[55] talks
about with children of alcoholics. Tec proves that teenagers who
felt that their parents did not care about their children's involvement with drugs accounted for the highest number of those involved in drug abuse.[56] The breakdown of generational boundaries often becomes necessary for survival. The children begin
satisfying the unmet emotional and physical (and too often,
sexual) needs of their parents to the extent that the "parentification flip-flop" takes place: the children become parents to
their own parents.

Unfortunately, parentification continues on from adolescence
through adult life. Unable to change his/her behavioral pattern of
fulfilling his parents' needs, the abuser, then, transmits to the next
generation an oppressive, role-confusing, inadequate family milieu.
The literature is complete with descriptions of family systems that
are so emotionally fused that any one member is unable to separate without an explosive "wrenching" of feelings.

A fourth theme is the family systems "role structure view," including the notion of coalitions and triangles. The family systems theorist views the basis of coalescents of a family as being a trading of complimentary needs and roles into a homeostatic balance. Abusive behavior in the parents, for example, meets the entire family system's need set; therefore, removal of the abusing behavior only means symptom displacement onto another family member. Abuse often is not limited to one child in the family.[57] When the abused child is removed, another child often becomes the next target. In the alcohol example given previously, clinicians have reported:

1. that in some families the well-being of other family members seems to be dependent upon the alcoholic member's continued drinking;
2. that in others, the nondrinking member began to decompensate as the drinking member got better;
3. that spouses often sought to sabotage treatment;
4. that drinking relapses frequently were influenced by the reentry of a recovered alcoholic into a family that had not changed.

Equilibrating mechanisms in a family may be employed to support "healthy" behavior, in order to create and support "sick" behavior. Behavior that is functional for the group may be dysfunctional in the view of outside observers. For some families, sobriety may be functional for the system; for others, continued drinking may be functional. Meeks,[58] Straus,[59] and Steinmetz[60] report that the same type of systems grew from negative and positive feedback in their explanation of violence in families.

Steinglass, Davis, and Berenson recently reported as a part of a study of interaction of conjointly hospitalized married couples that alcohol interaction patterns proved a stabilizing rather than a disruptive influence on the couples' relationships.[61] These interaction patterns represented attempts, albeit unsuccessful, to deal with family issues that could not otherwise be approached during sober periods. Spouse abuse interaction patterns are similarly reported as a stabilizing factor. Alcohol for such families becomes the organizing principle for interactional life and thus must be viewed as a stabilizer, albeit ruinous, and not a disrupter in family interactive life.

Most families can be characterized as having shifting alliances, splits, and triangles. Many coalitions, such as that of the marital team, are appropriate and necessary for a stable family structure. However, some families develop coalitions that are rigid and can produce problems with familiar imbalances. A coalition in this sense *is a situation in which two or more family members have a special bond or alliance that excludes or is different from other relationships within the family network.* Thus, this coalition may be seen when the wife of an alcoholic unconsciously, because of her own needs, seems to encourage her husband's alcoholism.[62] When the alcoholic is sober, the spouse decompensates and begins to show symptoms of neurotic disturbance into a competitive "one-upmenship" collusion game over control and cooperation in intimacy avoidance.

Kempe and Helfer note that prevalent passivity of the spouse of the child abuser as a factor in the abusing family.[63] Several authors (Boardman;[64] Elmer;[51] Gladston;[65] Gunn, et al.;[32] Holter and Friedman;[44] R. Smith;[66] Steele and Pollock;[39] Zalba[67]) reported the emotional unvariability or passivity and compliance of the spouse. Implicitly, both parents are involved in the abuse. One parent perpetuates the injury while the other parent keeps silent and, in doing so, lends passive support to the actively abusing parent. The parents of the abused child protect each other rather than the child; hence, a destructive triangle. A triangle is a specific type of "coalitionary" process that becomes a problem when there is a disturbance between two people that is handled by including a third person. Whenever a triangle is formed under these circumstances there is less chance of the original problem being resolved, and the disturbance will only intensify. As with the other family constellations previously described, coalitions and triangles become dysfunctional when they become fixed and rigid.

Steiner illustrated this family transactional triangle so well in his book, *Games Alcoholics Play*.[68] As part of these transactions, the alcoholic wife finds herself in distinctly conflicting roles, alternating between "rescuer," "persecutor," and "dummy" roles, and the bewildered spouse is caught in the crisis-prone cycle. This reversal of victim roles between the child and spouse is also supported by a report on children's treatment centers.[69] The classic triangular pathological situation is the scapegoat phenomenon. By providing a focal point for the projection of family discord, the scapegoat provides a channel for problem avoidance. In effect, the scapegoated family member serves a protected function for the family by providing a diversion, as well as helping insure greater unity through the family's shared projection defense system; the scapegoat cements the family bonds. This closeness would have to be relinquished with abstinence and the reentry of the abusing member. Often, the family member who is symptomatic may not be able to have influence in the family except by becoming more dysfunctional, thereby increasing the guilt of the family and making them more vulnerable to the needs of the sick member.

A fifth theme is the belief of the social class differential. A number of surveys have suggested that child abuse may be more prevalent among people of lower socioeconomic status (Gil;[70] Lysted;[71] Gregg and Elmer;[72] Johnson and Morse[47]). These surveys may be misleading due to the bias function of reporting systems. Hurt argues that middle-income families are poorly represented in hospital records and points out that private physicians may be less willing to report cases.[73] If so, it seems more likely that this phenomenon is not confined to a particular socioeconomic group and may be a problem in middle-income as well as lower-income families.[74] Indeed, Caffey states that child abusers can be found in all socioeconomic, ethnic, and religious groups.[75] He further argues that child-abusing parents have varying educational levels, and that they can be found in all parts of the country. As the reporting system for alcohol abuse had improved, the predominance of lower-class abuse had disappeared. The issue for both classes may be parenting skills and different class values.

A sixth theme is the sociocultural belief. Certain societal conditions may be encouraging alcohol, child abuse, etc. Similarly, some minority/socioeconomic/religious groups, because of the condition in society, may be more likely to engage in abusive behavior. Several investigators, among them Bandura,[76] Fontana,[77] and Gil[70] argue that this society sanctions such things as the use of physical force in child rearing and drug abuse. Bandura suggests that not only is violence sanctioned, but that society has developed a number of self-absolving practices that allow individuals to behave aggressively without fear of condemnation.[76] Another argument in which societal conditions and family violence abuse are related is presented by Bakan, who hypothesizes that such abuse has historically been related to the idea of maintaining a biological population-resource balance and has been one way of limiting population growth.[48]

LEGITIMIZATION

Much of the alcohol-family violence connection has been known for a long time. Until recently, the sensitivity of the subject matter has tended to provide barriers to identification, research, and treatment. The "uncleanliness" and complication of this problem arena have tended to repel professional study and intervention, often to the point of a projective downgrading of the field in favor of "cleaner" psychotherapies. As these problems have grown and affected more and more influential individuals, and as federal dollars have followed with appropriate concern, professionals have found new and renewed interest in this area.

Alcohol's association with family violence in western culture is not known, though the nature and extent of this association is not totally clear. Certainly further epidemiological and causal-linked research, as well as new treatment modalities, need to be created to match our new understanding of this association.

REFERENCES

1. Flanzer, J. Alcohol-abusing parents and their battered adolescents. In Galanter, M. (Ed.): *Currents in Alcoholism*, vol. VII. New York: Grune and Stratton, 1980.
2. Spieker, G., and Mousakitis, C.M. "Alcohol Abuse and Child Abuse and Neglect." Paper presented at the Alcohol and Drug Problems Association of North America, 27th annual meeting, New Orleans, Louisiana, Sept. 12-16, 1976.
3. Flanzer, J. The vicious circle of alcoholism and family violence. *Alcoholism*, (Jan.-Feb.): 30-32, 1981.
4. Sturkie, D.K., and Flanzer, J.P. An examination of two social work treatment models with abusive families. *Social Work Papers*, *16*: 53-62, 1981.

5. Snell, et al. The wife beater's wife: a study of family interactions. *Arch General Psychiatry, 11:*107-112, 1964.
6. Gelles, R.J. *The Violent Home.* Beverly Hills, California: Sage Publications, 1974.
7. McGaghy, C.H. Drinking and deviance disavowal: the case of child molesters. *Social Problems, 16 (1):*43-49, 1968.
8. Steinglass, P. Experimenting with family treatment approaches to alcoholism, 1950-1975: a review. *Family Process, 15 (1):*97-124, 1976.
9. Chafetz, M.E. Children of alcoholics. *Quarterly Journal of Studies on Alcohol, 32:*687-698, 1975.
10. Fine, E. et al. "Behavior Disorders in Children with Parental Alcoholism." Paper presented at the meeting of the National Council on Alcoholism, Milwaukee, Wisconsin, 1975.
11. Bosma, W.G. Alcoholism and teenagers. *Maryland State Medical Journal, 24:* pp. 24, 62, 68, 1975.
12. Schuckitt, M.A. Family history and half sibling research in alcoholism. *Annals of the New York Academy of Sciences, 215:*121-125, 1973.
13. Fox, R. "The Effect of Alcoholism on Children." New York, National Council on Alcoholism, 1972.
14. Golbetti, G. "Alcohol: A Family Affair." St. Louis National Congress of Parents and Teachers, 1973.
15. Booz, A. et al. *An Assessment of the Needs of and the Resources for Children of Alcoholic Parents* (NTIS). Rockville, Maryland, National Technical Information Service, National Institute Drug Abuse, 1976.
16. Hindman, M. Children of alcoholic parents. *Alcohol Health and Research World, 76 (6),* pp. 1-7, 1976.
17. Behling, D.W. "History of Alcohol Abuse in Child Abuse Cases Reported at Naval Regional Medical Center." Paper presented at the meeting of National Child Abuse Forum, Long Beach, California, June 1971.
18. Miketic, B. The influence of parental alcoholism in the development disturbance in children. *Alcoholism, 8:*135-139, 1972.
19. Grislain, J.R., de Berranger, M.P., de Perron, C., Brelet, G. "Child Abuse: Social and Legal Problems." *Journal of the American Medical Association,* 1968.
20. Popisil, Z., Turcin, K., Turcin, R., Alkolizam, i.e. 196. KZzlostavljante i Zapustarye malolgetnika. (Alcoholism and Article 196 of Criminal Law Abuse and Neglect of Minors). *New Ossihijatrija,* Zagreb, *16:* 49-53, 1968.
21. Nau, E. Kindesmisshandlung (Child Abuse), *Mschr. Kinderheilk, 115:* 192-194, 1967.
22. Ramee, F., and Michau, P. De Onelques Aspects de la Delinquance Secuell dans unDepartment de i-onset de la France. (Some Aspects of Sexual Offenses in a Province in Western France.) *Acta Med Leg Soc, 19:*79-85, 1966.
23. Virkkunen, M. Incest offenses and alcoholism. *Medicine Science and Law, 14:*124-128, 1974.

24. Tormes, Y.M. *Child Victims of Incest.* Denver, Colorado, American Humane Association.

25. Hanson, R., Shanks, R., and Sheldon, R. Patterns of communication in alcoholic married couples. *Psychiatric Quarterly, 42:*538-547, 1968.

26. Rae, J.B., and Drewery, J. Interpersonal patterns in alcoholic marriages. *British Journal of Psychiatry, 120:* 615-621, 1972.

27. Gerard, D., and Kornetsky, C. A social and psychiatric study of adolescent opiate addicts. *Psychiatric Quarterly, 28:*113-125, 1954.

28. Schwartzman, J. The addict, abstinence and the family. *American Journal of Psychiatry, 13 (2):*154-157, 1975.

29. Kempler, H. and McKennon, P. "Clinical Observations and Belief Family Therapy of Drug Abusing Adolescents and Their Families." Paper presented at the 52nd meeting of the American Orthopsychiatric Association, Washington, D. C., 1975.

30. Jackson, J.K. The adjustment of the family to the crisis of alcoholism. *Quarterly Journal of Studies on Alcoholism, 15:*562-586, 1964.

31. Bailey, M.B. "Alcoholism and Family Casework: Theory and Practice." *Community Council of Greater New York,* New York, 1968.

32. Gunn, A.I. The neglected child. *Nursing Times, 66 (30):*946-947, 1970.

33. Smith, S., Hanson, R., and Noble, S. Parents of battered babies: a controlled study. *British Medical Journal, 4:*388-391, 1973.

34. Kempe, D.H., and Helfer, R.E. (Eds.) *Helping the Battered Child and His Family,* Philadelphia, J.B. Lippincott and Company, 1972.

35. Alexander, B., and Dibb, S. Opiate addicts and their parents. *Family Process, 14:*499-514, 1975.

36. Spinetta, J.J., and Rigler, D. The child abusing parent: a psychological review. *Psychological Bulletin, 4:*296-304, 1972.

37. Baher, E. et al. *At Risk: An Account of the Work of the Battered Child Research Department.* Boston, Routledge and Kegan Paul, 1976.

38. DeLissovoy, V. Child care by adolescent parents. *Children Today, 2 (4):* 22-25, 1973.

39. Steele, B., and Pollock, C. "A Psychiatric Study of Parents Who Abuse Infants and Small Children," *Helping the Battered Child and His Family.* Philadelphia, Lippincott, (In Kempe & Helfer, (Eds.) 1972. op.cit.

40. Gregg, G.S. Infant Trauma. *American Family Physician, 3:*101-105, 1971.

41. Burglass, N. Parents with emotional problems. *Nursing Times, 67:* 1000-1001, 1971.

42. Straus, M. A general systems theory approach to a theory of violence between family members. *Social Science Information, 12:*105-125, 1972.

43. Laury, G.V. The battered child syndrome: parental motivation, clinical aspects. *Bulletin of the New York Academy of Medicine, 46 (9):* 676-685, 1970.

44. Holter, J., and Friedman, S. Child abuse: early casefinding in the emergency department. *Pediatrics, 42 (1):*128-138, 1968.

45. Bullard, D. et al. Failure-to-thrive in the neglected child. *American Journal of Orthopedics, 37 (4):*680-690, 1967.

46. Togut, M. et al. Psychological exploration of the nonorganic failure-to-thrive syndrome. *Developmental Medicine and Child Neurology, 11:* 601-607, 1969.

47. Johnson, B., and Morse, H.A. Injured children and their parents. *Children, 15 (4):*147-152, 1968.

48. Bakan, D. *Slaughter of the Innocents.* San Francisco, Jossey-Bass, 1971.

49. Jackson, J.K. The adjustment of the family to the crisis of alcoholism. *Quarterly Journal of Studies on Alcoholism, 15:*562-586, 1964.

50. Callaghan, K.A., and Fotheringham, B.J. Practical management of the battered baby syndrome. *Medical Journal of Australia* (Sydney), *1:*1282-1284, 1970.

51. Elmer, E. Child abuse: a symptom of family crisis. In Pavenstedt, E., and Mernard, U. (Eds.): *Crises of Family Disorganization.* New York, Behavioral Publishers, pp. 51-58, 1971.

52. Evans, S., Reinhart, J. and Succor, R. "Failure To Thrive: A Study of 45 Children and Their Families." *American Academy of Child Psychiatry Journal, 2:*440-457, 1972.

53. Hecht, M. Children of alcoholics. *American Journal of Nursing, 73:* pp. 1764-1767, 1973.

54. Seldin, M. The family of the addict: a review of the literature. *The International Journal of the Addictions, 7 (1):*97-107, 1972.

55. Burke, D. Some contemporary issues in child development and the children of alcoholic parents. *New York Academy of Science Annuals, 214:* pp. 189-197, 1972.

56. Tec, N. Family therapy and drug abuse. *International Pharmacopsychiatry, 7 (1-4):*153-156, 1972.

57. Skinner, A., and Castle, R. *Seventy-eight Battered Children: A Retrospective Study.* London, England, National Society for the Prevention of Cruelty to Children, 1969.

58. Meeks, D.E. Family therapy. In Turter, R., and Sugarman, A. (Eds): *Alcoholism: Interdisciplinary Approaches to an Enduring Problem,* London, England, Adison-Wesley, 1976.

59. Straus, M. Cultural and social organizational influences on violence between family members. In Prince, R., and Barried, D. (Eds.): *Configurations: Biological and Cultural Factors in Sexuality and Family Life.* New York, D.C. Heath, Lexington Books, pp. 53-69, 1974.

60. Steinmetz, S.K., and Straus, M.A. *Violence in the Family.* New York, Dod, Mean and Company, 1974.

61. Steinglass, P., Davis, D.I. and Berenson, D. Observations of conjointly hospitalized alcoholic couples during sobriety and intoxication. *Family Process, 16 (1):*1-15, 1977.

62. Futterman, S. Personality trends in wives of alcoholics. *Journal of Psychiatric Social Work, 23:* pp. 37-41, October 23, 1953.

63. Kempe, C., and Helfer, R. (Eds.) *Helping the Battered Child and His Family*, Philadelphia, Lippincott, 1972.

64. Boardman, J. Who insures the child's right to health? *Child Welfare, 43 (3):* 120-124, 1963.

65. Gladston, R. Dysfunctioning of parenting: the battered child, the neglected child, the exploited child. In Howells, J. (Ed.) *Modern Perspective on International Child Psychiatry*, New York, Brunner-Mazel, pp. 571-588, 1971.

66. Smith, R.C. New ways to help battering parents. *Today's Health, 51 (1):* 57-64, 1973.

67. Zalba, S.R. The abused child II: a typology for classification and treatment. *Social Work, 12 (1):* 70-79, 1967.

68. Steiner, C. *Games Alcoholics Play.* New York, Grove Press, 1971.

69. Holmes, M. et al. *The Impact of the Parent-Child Centers on Parents: A Preliminary Report.* New York, Center for Community Research, 1973.

70. Gil, D.G. *Violence Against Children: Physical Child Abuse in the United States.* Cambridge, Massachusetts, Harvard University Press, 1970.

71. Lysted, M.H. Violence at home: a review of the literature. *American Journal of Orthopsychiatry, 45:* pp. 328-345, 1975.

72. Gregg, G.S., and Elmer, E. Infant injuries: accident or abuse? *Pediatrics, 44:* 434-439, 1969.

73. Hurt, M. *Child Abuse and Neglect: A Report on the Status of the Research.* U.S. Department of Health, Education and Welfare, Office of Human Development, Office of Child Development, Children's Bureau DHEW Publication No. (OHD) 74-20, 1975.

74. Wasserman, S. The abused parent of the abused child. *Children,* (September-October), *14 (5):* pp. 159-175, 1967.

75. Caffey, J., Silverman, F., Kempe, C., Venters, H., and Leonard, M. Child battery: seek and save. *Medical World News, 13 (22):* pp. 21-33, 1972.

76. Bandura, A. Institutionally sanctioned violence. *Journal of Child Psychology, 2 (3):* 23, 1973.

77. Fontana, V.J. Battered children. *New England Journal of Medicine, 289 (19):* 1044, 1973.

Chapter 5

SOCIAL COMPETENCE, FAMILY VIOLENCE, AND PROBLEM DRINKING

John J. Steffen

This chapter represents an initial attempt to develop a model of the relations between problem drinking and family violence from the perspective of cognitive social learning theory — a currently dominant theoretical perspective within clinical and social psychology (Bandura, 1977; Mischel, 1973). The basic premise is that family violence, problem drinking, and their conjoint occurrence can be best understood from a perspective that considers them socially learned phenomena. My contention is that both familial violence and problem drinking are acquired patterns of social interaction, and that neither can be meaningfully studied or understood without reference to the interpersonal context within which they occur. In this discussion the organismic/genetic factors considered to play a role in the occurrence of both phenomena will be viewed as predisposing and not potentiating determinants of these forms of social behavior. Primary emphasis will be placed upon the potentiation of violence and problem drinking by cognitive and environmental determinants. The intent is not to deny the importance of organismic variables, but rather to identify the possible psychological variables that may contribute to the joint tragedies of family violence and problem drinking.

51

The following section will present a brief discussion of cognitive social learning theory with regard to the development of social competencies. To this end, both problem drinking and violent behavior will be viewed as socially incompetent behaviors. This section will also document the importance of the social context as the primary frame from which to view both phenomena. This discussion will serve as a prelude to an analysis of the conditions that contribute to the acquisition, performance, and maintenance of both patterns of interaction. Thus, violent behavior and problem drinking will be viewed as interactional phenomena that are developed and maintained by the transactions an individual accomplishes within his environment. A final section will pose a series of research questions that are derived from the preceding analyses. These questions are intended to both stimulate discussion and point to potentially fruitful areas of inquiry.

SOCIAL COMPETENCE AND COGNITIVE
SOCIAL LEARNING THEORY

Previous theories of human learning, growth, and development have placed a heavy emphasis upon either organismic or environmental processes as the major determinant of human behavior. Organismic theories of development postulate an intraindividual system of personality formation that, depending upon the particular theorist, fixes development as an inevitable process sometime within the first three years of life. Thus, the individual's later adult development is seen as a *fait accompli* in early childhood. Such positions deemphasize the role of environmental factors as determinants of later-life learning. Opposed to this position is the one held by environmentalists, who hold with Locke, that the infant (and presumably the adult) is a tabula rasa that the environment can shape into any form. For these theorists, experience and learning play the major role in determining human behavior. Both positions hold in common a relatively rigid conception of learning. At the extreme, each denies the importance of the other for development. When forced into a compromise, the picture of a mutual process of organismic and environmental determination is presented where the individual alternates between being a slave to nature or to nurture. Kuhn (1978) has characterized all three systems as mechanistic ones, since there is a presumed invariant, or mechanical, cause-effect relation between organismic and/or environmental conditions and the person. Recent theoretical positions within developmental, social, and clinical psychology have questioned this invariant relation between nurture, nature, and the person, suggesting that a mutual, reciprocally dynamic influencing process may well provide a more adequate explanation of how people become who they are. Cognitive social learning theory, as recently elaborated by Bandura (1977, 1978), provides a perspective to the acquisition of social behavior and frees the individual from the chains of his nature and nurture and allows him to fully participate in the process of learning. Figure 5-1 presents a schematic of the cognitive social learning model of the forces that determine an individual's social behavior. Three processes are presumed to operate in a reciprocally dynamic fashion upon one another: person, environment, and behavior. The term "reciprocally dynamic" refers to the major assumption that each process influences and is influenced by one another. The "person" processes refer to those factors that reside within an individual: her unique biological-physiological constitution, as well as all those past learning experiences that she presently embodies. These processes are viewed as those conditions that an individual brings with herself into any novel environment and have been generally described as both the physical and characterological attributes of the individual. The "environmental" processes refer to those aspects of the individual's social context that influence her actions or behavior at the moment they are displayed. A rather long tradition of research within psychology has documented the impact of environmental factors upon an individual's moment-to-moment behavior (Mischel, 1968, 1973; Skinner, 1958). The "behavior" process represents the influence of the individual's own actions upon what constitutes her current intrapersonal and interpersonal context. Thus, the individual's actions are seen as not just influenced by the context within which they are acting, but also as a major factor that influences the context as well (Steffen, forthcoming). The individual's actions help create the environment in which she acts. Her behavior helps to provide meaning to whatever social context she performs in. Further,

her actions help shape her more enduring personological characteristics, in that they allow her to be exposed to different experiences within the environment.

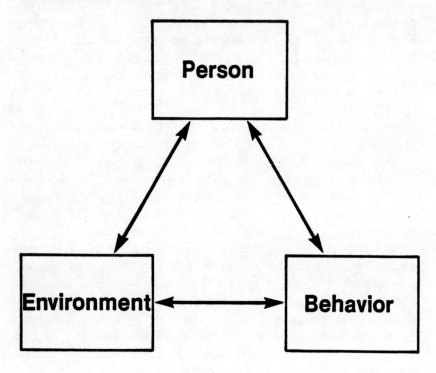

Figure 5-1

The cognitive social learning model of social competence assumes that these three factors play the major role in determining
the individual's characteristic activity within his environment.
In this regard, characteristic modes of action are seen as arising
from the individual's experiences within the environment. Thus,
behavior patterns are acquired as the result of social learning,
which takes as its major form the observations of how the others
in the individual's world conduct themselves under similiar circumstances. While other modes of learning may play a role in the
individual's acquisition of competent patterns of behaving, the influence of observational or modeling processes are seen as paramount.

One major assumption within this model is that there is a fairly strong influence on the individual's acquisition and display of competent behavior by the social context. Indeed, individuals may well appear incompetent in certain contexts and competent in others (Erickson and Schultz, 1977), with the prevailing contextual conditions playing an important role in determining both the interpretation of the actions as competent or not, as well as setting the occasion for competent action to occur.

While there is considerable contention among investigators of social competence as to what precisely constitutes competent comportment, a general model may be offered that can be applied to an analysis of family violence and problem drinking. To this end, competent behavior can be seen as a series of self-adjusting actions that an individual displays within a particular context that represent, for the individual, his or her own best attempts to maximize personally satisfying, as well as minimize unsatisfying, outcomes. While this definition is purposely vague, it can be readily applied to most forms of social behavior. Several components of this definition must be explained before we proceed with our analysis. First, "series of self-adjusting" actions refers to the physical (behavior) *and* cognitive (person) actions of the individual within the social context. Mischel (1973), among others (Kelly, 1955; O'Banion and Arkowitz, 1978; Steffen, forthcoming; Steffen and Reckman, 1978), postulates certain cognitive competencies that predispose an individual to competent social behavior. Foremost among these are two: cognitive construal and behavioral enactment competencies. Cognitive construal competence refers to the individual's ability to assess accurately the meaning of the social context. This requires a multiphasic processing of the information contained within the context and relies upon the individual's prior experiences under similar circumstances to the ones he currently finds himself in. Deficiencies in this regard may lead an individual to misunderstand the context and what particular actions are required under those circumstances. For example, a parent may come to interpret a child's incessant crying as "being a pest" and act in a fashion that assumes a certain pattern of behavior will remedy the crying. Another parent, however, may interpret the same crying as needing attention and may also act accordingly. The first interpretation may well lead a parent to engage in physical violence, while the second to expressions of tenderness, depending upon the parents' behavioral enactment competence. This latter competence refers to the parents' store of information with regard to "how to act" under the interpreted conditions. Some parents may have learned from past experiences that the way to act when a child is being a pest is to hit him. Others may have learned that the thing to do is to ignore her. Likewise, the interpretation of needing attention may evoke a response of feeding, cuddling, diaper changing, or ignoring, depending upon the parents' own repertoire of likely actions. We can see from these brief examples that the actions an individual engages in are rather complex and depend, in a large part, upon what past experiences have taught the person to do under the contextual circumstances.

The second aspect we must consider with regard to competence is the role of the social context. Just as an individual cannot act in isolation from some contextual setting, the setting itself has no meaning without reference to how people act in it (Steffen, forthcoming). This would imply, for example, that one could not understand the phenomena of family violence or problem drinking without reference to the contextual/environmental conditions that serve as their setting. However, the current definition of context refers to more than the physical and social elements that constitute a context. The understanding of the context, as it is held by the participants, is as important as its physical reality. This fact was alluded to in the previous discussion of the patterns of action that constitute competence. Some recent work by Burgess (1979) and his colleagues at Pennsylvania State University on child abuse are relevant to this discussion. In brief, Burgess has found that different patterns of interaction can differentiate between abusing and nonabusing families, i.e., the particular behaviors the abusing parent exhibits toward the abused child cannot alone explain whether or not violence will occur. The entire family system must be observed, since it appears that there are certain characteristic patterns exhibited by the other members in a child-abusing family. From the current perspective, this would suggest that there is a qualitative difference in the social contexts of abusing and non-abusive families. While Burgess and his colleagues have not yet made attempts to identify the unique contextual interpretations made by abused and abusive families, such an effort would seem to be important to understand how both parents and child understand family violence.

The final aspect of the definition of competence refers to the particular outcome of the individual's actions. It is assumed that all people strive to maintain some form of satisfaction from their social encounters. It is now a truism within the social sciences, however, that all individuals do not value the same things. Indeed, several behavioral researchers have shown that some people consider certain events as pleasurable that most would consider aversive. This idiosyncracy can often lead to rather bizarre consequences. Indeed, Laing and Esterson (1964) have documented the often distasteful and bizarre social consequences inherent in schizophrenic families. Even in nonschizophrenic families certain types of interactions may come to be valued by its members that would be considered abusive in others. Almost every mental health professional working with children can recall at least one child who had come to equate "spanking" with "love," because that was the interpretation the child's parents gave to the spanking.

Before proceeding with our analysis of family violence and problem drinking, several points should be emphasized concerning the current model. First, social behavior cannot be fully understood without reference to the context within which it occurs. This assumes, then, that we cannot understand the behavior of a problem drinker or a physical abuser without consideration of the family system within which the behavior is displayed. Second, all social behavior is seen as a function of reciprocal relation among the determinants of the individual's context (environment), actions (behavior), and personal characteristics (person). Thus, a search for the causes of physical or alcohol abuse in the individual, her behavior, or her environment alone will provide only an incomplete understanding of those problems. Finally, an individual's unique construal of her family system must be considered, as well as the interrelation among the members of that system. This point, long emphasized by adherents of family therapy (Haley, 1963; Jackson, 1959; Satir, 1964), is particularly relevant in the current concerns of family violence and alcohol abuse and, while inherent in the reciprocally dynamic model cited above, must be emphasized. Research on family violence has started to reveal certain characteristic patterns of action among all family members in child abuse families. The individual's unique interpretation of those actions, as well as the mutual dependencies of family members' behaviors upon other members' behavior, must be explored.

FAMILY VIOLENCE

The once sacrosanct boundaries of American families have been invaded by interviewers, television cameras, and social scientists. Closer examination of the family has revealed that characters far more sinister than those dreamt of by Charles Addams live within the family dwelling. While we have been aware for a long time that the lemonade freshness of a Norman Rockwell family was more artistic fantasy than everyday reality, Americans have been shocked by the reports of journalists and social scientists documenting the psychological and physical abuse rampant in American homes. Child abuse, wife abuse, sibling abuse, incest, and parricide are now as frequent referents to the American family as hot dogs, apple pie, and Sunday visits to grandma once were. In fact, grandma and grandpa are now more likely to be seen as abused themselves than visited on Sundays.

Have we become a violent society with vestiges of our increasing violence creeping into the family health? Doomsayers would do well to point to the recent rash of national and international assassinations of political leaders and hostages and the apparent increase of mass slayings to support such a point. Even as I write this chapter, a tragic case of child abuse, resulting in the death of a seven-year-old child, has been reported by the local media. The child was beaten unconscious by his mother and her boyfriend, who then stuffed thirty-five red peppers down his throat. The mother claimed that this was done because the child ate a piece of cheese on a day of fasting, which was against her religious custom. We are all struck by the senselessness of such crimes, whether they happen to national figures, the child next door, or someone in the newspaper.

But finding no sense in such wanton destruction of human life should impel us to ask probing questions about such forms of family violence. The murder of a child by his own mother may be rare; however, one must ask how much and in what form does violence occur in our families. First, one must define the meaning of violence. In considering family violence we think of repeated occurrences of physical abuse to a degree that the victim and victimizer come to the attention of civil authorities. However, this form of violence may well represent only a small fraction of the abuse that occurs inside the home. Can we, for example, deny that constant neglect and inconsistent nurturing do not, themselves, represent a less severe degree of abuse than a broken arm or a cigarette burn on the leg? For the abused individual, a psychological injury is as real and damaging as a physical one. Social scientists, who are fond of quantifying reality, find it difficult to make such a judgment. Indeed, one contention of this chapter is that psychological violence within the family must be considered as real and damaging as physical violence. While the sequelae of psychological injuries are not as readily apparent as those of physical injuries, their long-term effect upon the integrity of the person may be as severe.

From the perspective of the current cognitive social learning model of socially competent behavior, both physical and psychological violence are seen as emanating from a common core of conditions. To this end, violence can be seen as an interactional phenomena. In other words, it occurs between two or more individuals. For violence within the family, a further consideration is added: the two or more individuals have a past history of interaction, which, in all likelihood, has an influence upon their current patterns of interaction. In this model, then, two actors are seen as engaging in a continuing encounter where one does some form of psychological and/or physical harm to the other. For the victimizer, certain predisposing person variables must be present, in association with certain environmental conditions, before the violent behavior is displayed. While the exact nature of these predisposing conditions is not yet clear, we do know from previous investigations that abusive individuals are more likely to have been abused themselves as children. This would suggest, if one accepts the view that most behavior is observationally acquired, that the seeds of violence were planted in the victimizer's youth through the victimizer's repeated exposure to violent acts within the family. Thus, this individual learned that, under certain circumstances, violence is the only recourse to action. However, additional research has shown that the victim, himself, is somewhat different from other family members in his style of interacting. This finding suggests that the victim of violence contributes, in part, to the abusive encounter. This is not to suggest that the victim be blamed for his ill fate (Ryan, 1971), rather, that there is a certain reciprocity between the victim and victimizer that must be understood. Neither actor is fully to be blamed for the violent encounter, although the burden of guilt must rest upon the instigator of the violence.

This burden of guilt, however, is the result of the instigator's characteristic response to the contextual condition that produced the violence. Thus, the victimizer's construal and behavioral enactment competencies play a role in determining the action she will engage in. If she has a limited repertoire of action, and some form of violent action is included in her repetoire, then she is more likely to engage in such a pattern of action under the appropriate circumstances. If she has no other personally satisfying alternative, she will engage in an abusive action. The resort to psychological and/or physical abuse in an encounter is viewed as socially incompetent by the force of the ultimate consequences such actions evoke. The individual who engages in abusive behavior, then, can be seen as one who has a limited repertoire of actions available to him under the circumstances that call for some form of action. Further, this individual, as noted previously, may well misread the context to call for violent behavior and interpret a child's crying as an annoyance to be quieted in any way. While to most nonviolent individuals certain alternative actions would be suggested by the circumstances that drive others to violence, those violent individuals have only a limited number of responses available to them.

In conclusion, violent behavior can be viewed as a deficient form of social behavior. The nature of this deficiency stems from the violent individual's misperception of the situation or his limited social repertoire. Further, the commission of violent behavior represents a small part in an ongoing series of activities that characterize the encounter between victim and victimizer. This last point underscores the necessity to evaluate all conditions that prevail at the time of the violent action.

PROBLEM DRINKING

A similar set of circumstances can be described to apply to the individual who abuses alcohol. In this regard, problem drinking can be seen to evolve as the result of a certain set of contextual conditions that drive a person to abuse alcohol; thus, individuals have learned certain characteristic modes of response to environmental conditions. Among those patterns may exist the tendency to consume large quantities of beverage alcohol. As Steffen and Nathan (1977) have noted:

> Although fully articulated behavioral theories of alcoholism etiology have not yet evolved, social learning theory (Bandura, 1969; Mischel, 1973) provides important initial direction for a behavioral explanation of chronic alcohol abuse.
>
> The social learning perspective presumes that the alcoholic individual's family served and serves as a prime focus for development of his/her maladaptive drinking practices. It is from the family — later from the peer group as well — that society's rules governing alcohol consumption are acquired. Via the same mode of behavior transmission, in turn, the person who is to become an alcohol abuser learns that alcohol consumption can serve as an effective response to stressful or otherwise aversive experiences. According to this view, excessive alcohol consumption eventually becomes such an individual's major coping response to stress. This fact, coupled with increasing tolerance and physiologic addiction to alcohol, leads the alcoholic into chronic, destructive physical and psychological dependence on alcohol. Further consequences of repeated excessive alcohol consumption, including alcohol withdrawal symptoms, vocational instability, alcohol-related physical disease, and marital and familial disequilibrium, then may themselves come to serve as stressful stimuli which maintain the cycle of alcoholism.
>
> In other words, social learning theory posits that excessive drinking is a learned phenomenon maintained by stress reduction, peer influence, and physical dependence. In addition, the consequences of drinking add further stress in the form of employment, marital, and familial disturbance. Although the relationships among these determinants of alcoholism are quite complex and hence beyond the scope of this chapter, they suggest the range of factors that must be considered in the design of behavioral treatment programs for alcoholism.

These conditions that arise to promote abusive drinking often come to promote violence within the family. In this regard, there may well exist a common set of person and environmental conditions that lead people to engage in physically abusive behavior while under the influence of alcohol. However, the importance of the social context must be emphasized in this regard. MacAndrew and Edgerton (1969) have written quite eloquently on this matter. They point out that cross-cultural studies in the area of alcohol do not substantiate the view that alcohol may serve as a releaser for the more base patterns of human action. In their work on drunken comportment, they cite example after example substantiating the fact that alcohol, in most cultures, has come to serve as a signal for the individual to engage in patterns of action generally proscribed under conditions of sobriety; thus, promiscuous love is as likely to ensue as promiscuous violence. While many may draw their analysis to suggest that alcohol may serve as a universal inhibitor of usual societal constraints for appropriate action, they conclude that alcohol abuse merely signals the occurrence of a removal of constraints, given the particular contextual circumstances. In their book, they cite the example of a missionary in Africa who described a rather unusual encounter. It was common knowledge within this society in which the missionary dwelt that one member of the tribe was given to murderous impulses when he had consumed alcohol. Numerous tales were told about the heads of innocents that had fallen at the machete of the drunkenly crazy warrior. One day, while the missionary was walking down a path in the jungle, several tribesmen came running frantically in the opposite direction. Apparently, the murderous warrior had had too much to drink that day and had exclaimed that he would remove anyone's head that came in his way. Justifiably terrified, the missionary prepared to move in a direction opposite to the one he had been going. Unfortunately, as he turned, he found himself face to face with the drunkenly mad warrior who was now menacingly waving his machete about. As the story goes, the mad warrior, upon seeing the missionary, ceased his drunken screams and said, "Good afternoon, father" and continued on his way, waving his machete and screaming. MacAndrew and Edgerton (1966) make the point, by this example, that often societal conditions predispose individuals to act in certain ways under the influence of alcohol. This example should serve to represent a suggestion concerning the impact of alcohol upon violent behavior in the family. Thus, there must be certain conditions present within the family of the problem drinker that predispose him to violence. Further, he must confront a set of circumstances that lead him to violence.

SUGGESTIONS FOR RESEARCH

While the previous discussions have been quite tentative with regard to the causes and cures of familial violence, so too the current state of knowledge in this area must be considered quite tentative and in need of further investigation. Several areas of inquiry must be opened before we can begin to acknowledge even minimal advances in this regard. First, certain basic conditions must be agreed upon for the occurrence of violence in families. It was noted earlier that psychological as well as physical violence must be included in any consideration of violent forms of interaction. The range of injustice that one individual may enact upon another must be clearly specified, otherwise we may only remain aware of only the most dramatic and newsworthy cases of violence.

Second, once identified, violence-prone families must be studied in-depth in the same manner that Burgess applied to his abusive families. However, we must pay more attention to what certain actions mean within families than Burgess has accomplished. That is, while certain actions may appear to be negative to an outsider, familial conditions may well be such that those actions are considered to be positive and rewarding within the limits of the family under consideration. Without appearing to be a liberal soothsayer, I must urge that we as social scientists take the time to understand what drove the victimizer to engage in his violent act. Perhaps if we understood what unique understanding led a woman to participate in the beating of her own child, we could come to understand what might drive other mothers and fathers to act accordingly.

Third, in viewing these violent actions as social skill deficits, I am suggesting that we attempt remediation efforts at a very basic level. While most Americans have been adequately prepared to handle the stresses of family life, many have not. They may have learned that a crying child should be silenced in any way possible,

or that a child who violates religious proscriptions must be punished. These parents must be exposed to alternative methods of
family comportment. While beating a child into a state of un-
consciousness may silence her, other methods also work. Those
parents who view physical and psychological abuse as *the* method
of parenting must be taught alternative methods.

Finally, lest this chapter be viewed as a Pollyannaish report of
a social scientist bent upon remedying societal problems, my last
recommendation represents the most difficult one to pursue, but
probably the most realistic one as well: we must pool our resources to find some avenues into the American family. While
Dr. Spock and the Louds may well have had an influence upon our
child-rearing activities, some form of social action is necessary to
bring about a change in the violent activities that occur within the
confines of the family. I personally find any form of governmental legislation with regard to the family and its creation as distasteful, however, any alternative method of control appears, at
the present, to be unsatisfactory. To this end, we should devote a
considerable amount of our resources toward effective family and
parent education. I do not refer here to the continuation of ineffective methods of instruction. Rather, I refer to those methods
of education that prove quite effective in their application. In
this regard, several approaches toward marital and parent training
within my speciality area, behavior therapy and modification, have
proven to be quite effective in teaching individuals alternative
means of family interaction to the ones they too readily employ.
While many social critics may blanch at such methods, they do
hold considerable promise for fostering more humane and rewarding encounters within the family.

REFERENCES

Bandura, A. *Principles of Behavior Modification.* New York, Holt, 1969.
Bandura, A. Self efficacy: Toward a unifying theory of behavioral change.
    Psychological Review, 84: 191-215, 1977.
Bandura, A. The self-system in reciprocal determinism. *American Psycholo-
    gist, 33:* 344-358, 1978.
Burgess, R.L. Child abuse: A social interactional analysis, In Lahey, B.B.,
    and Kazdin, A.E. (Eds.), *Advances in Clinical Child Psychology, vol.2.*
    New York, Plenum, 1979.

Erickson, F., and Schultz, J.J. When is a context? Some issues and methods in the analysis of social competence. *Quarterly Newsletter of the Institute for Comparative Human Development, 1*(2): 5-10, 1977.

Haley, J. *Strategies of Psychotherapy.* New York, Grune and Stratton, 1963.

Jackson, D.D. Family interaction, family homeostasis and some implications for conjoint family therapy. In Masserman, J. (Ed.), *Individual and Familial Dynamics.* New York, Grune and Stratton, 1959.

Kelly, G.A. *The Psychology of Personal Constructs. Volume 1: A Theory of Personality.* New York, Norton, 1955.

Kuhn, D. Mechanisms of cognitive and social development: One psychology or two? *Human Development, 21:* 92-118, 1978.

Laing, R.D., and Esterson, A. *Sanity, Madness, and the Family.* New York, Basic Books, 1964.

MacAndrew, C., and Edgerton, R.B. *Drunken Comportment: A Social Explanation.* Chicago, Aldine, 1969.

Mischel, W. *Personality and Assessment.* New York, Wiley, 1968.

Mischel, W. Toward a cognitive social learning reconceptualization of personality. *Psychological Review, 80:* 740-754, 1973.

O'Banion, K., and Arkowitz, H. Social anxiety and selective memory for affective information about the self. *Social Behavior and Personality, 5:* 321-328, 1977.

Ryan, W. *Blaming the Victim.* New York, Vintage, 1971.

Satir, V. *Conjoint Family Therapy.* Palo Alto, California, Science and Behavior Books, 1964.

Skinner, B.G. *The Behavior of Organisms.* New York, Appleton-Century, 1938.

Steffen, J.J. *Measuring Social Interaction Competence.* New York, Praeger, forthcoming.

Steffen, J.J., and Nathan, P.E. Treatment of alcoholism. In Harris, G.G., (Ed.), *The Group Treatment of Human Problems: A Social Learning Approach.* New York, Grune and Stratton, 1977.

Steffen, J.J., and Reckman, R.F. Selective perception and interpretation of interpersonal cues in dyadic interaction. *Journal of Psychology, 99:* 245-248. 1978.

Chapter 6
A SOCIOLOGICAL PERSPECTIVE ON
THE CONTROL OF VIOLENCE
IN FAMILIES
Mark Krain

Family violence, which, for purposes of this chapter, refers to child abuse, spouse abuse, and abuse of elderly family members, is surely the most ignoble of phenomena connected with the study of the family. The topic provokes a rare degree of reproachfulness in the minds of laymen and experts. In discussions in my course on the sociology of the family, I have seen the same degree of vehement contempt for child beaters and wife beaters that I have seen in my social problems course in connection with torturers. In one course, a student heatedly advocated public amputation of a hand for child beaters, as the Arabs do for thievery, to prevent the crime. We react to the criminal as much as, or even more so, to the crime. The perpetrator of an act of family violence is assumed to be bad or mad; punishment or therapy is assumed to be the remedy. Expanded views of the problem frequently go beyond reacting to the perpetrator to consider more complex factors of the relationship between the perpetrator and the victim, and perhaps even additional parties to the situation. This chapter takes the position that there is yet more to the story than this. It will be argued that in historical context the present-day structure of the American family is closed to external influence to an unprecedented degree.   This closure engenders a radical privacy within which nonnormative violence can occur unchecked. Policies and treatment interventions aimed at controlling or preventing family violence must recognize this structural aspect of the problem.   Although it is not the intent of this chapter to seek to advance a single-factor theory of the family violence, it takes the position that the ultimate control of family violence lies in structural manipulation to provide checks on the use of violence. This point will be explained more fully after some general perspectives on violence and its control are explored.

CONFLICT AND EXCHANGE THEORY

Sociological thought is most heavily oriented toward consensus models of social process. Such models emphasize order and harmony, as they presuppose agreement on goals within groups, and they presuppose agreement on behavior that constitutes the means to the achievement of those goals. If such models were valid, violence would indeed be rare. At the same time there are at least two perspectives in sociological thought that might predict the awesome amount of family violence of which we are now aware. They might even suggest that even greater levels of family violence are yet to be discovered. These perspectives are *conflict theory* and *exchange theory*.

Conflict theory is the sociological perspective that is most clearly drawn in contrast to the consensus perspective. It proceeds from the assumption that conflict and combativeness, rather than agreement, order, and harmony, is the normal state of things. Power play, constant subversion of rules, or inability to establish rules in the first place is the prevailing mode of existence. What is to be explained in this way of viewing things is the nature of constraints imposed by culture and social institutions that account for any absence of totally pandemic violence that may be found. In this perspective the question of madness or badness is beside the point.   Both are considered to be thoroughly distributed among all components of the population: we are all mad and/or bad. Given this, what forces us to behave in a reasonably civil manner? What constraints are absent, or deficient, when people are being violent?

Exchange and game theories are a group of related perspectives that also provide for the conceptualization of high levels of violence. These perspectives emphasize calculation of benefit and advantage. The normal state of affairs is bargaining, negotiation, and reciprocation. This perspective points out that exchanges of hurts, injuries, and malevolence are every bit as likely as exchanges of gifts, help, and benevolence. What is to be explained here are the conditions under which "bribery" or "payoff" models do not work and "coercion" or "retribution" models do. The question of madness or badness is irrelevent in this perspective. Violence is viewed as rational and has real profit for its practitioners. The issues here are ones of the regulation of the market and the terms of trade. Can victims of violence find ways of dealing with perpetrators in "fair trade" regulated markets, and can they up the cost of the use of violence?

Both of these perspectives allow us to begin to look at family violence as an expectable and normal (one shudders to use these terms!) component of family life even at the now known high incidence levels. Both perspectives focus attention away from the perpetrator of violence, even when considered in context of the interactional and cyclic character of the behavior sequences within which violence occurs. The two perspectives outlined above both see that the adoption of policies of violence utilization by family members are not manipulable by therapy, training, resocialization, acquisition of competencies, or any other strategy aimed at an effect on the motivational or cognitive faculties of individuals. Similarly, conceptualizations of sequences of victim-perpetrator interaction cycles, while they have the advantage of identifying a wider range of factors and influences that have a bearing on the pattern of violent acts, do not articulate the problem in ways that afford prime clues on how to control the violence. In order to move toward perspectives on the control of family violence a very abstract idea of violence control must first be considered.

NORMATIVE MATRIX

All behavior occurs with reference to a *normative matrix*. This is to say that all behavior is at least subject to evaluation by self and observers, in terms of roles and standards existing in culture and society, which rate the acceptability of that behavior. These rules and standards may be society-wide or they may be limited to subcultures and given groups. One's behavior is most likely to be controlled by this normative matrix when it is observed by others, at least one of whom is in a position to take some kind of action if the behavior is contrary to rules and standards. Conversely, behavior is least likely to be controlled when the behaving person is the only one who is aware of the behavior and is the only one who decides upon acceptability. Where the behavior involves another person, as does violence which involves a perpetrator and a victim, the perpetrator's behavior is least likely to be controlled when the victim can be compelled not to disclose the occurrence of violence. The victim in such a case is not an observer in a position to react normatively.

Two issues arise at this point. First is the *content* of the normative matrix. What does it say about violence, the behavior we are concerned with, and family violence in particular? Second is the *bearing* of the normative matrix. To what extent are individuals subjected to its control? To what extent are situations likely to include violent acts subject to observation by agents who are in a position to take action against it?

The content issue is mainly a question of what violence is acceptable. There is variability between societies and within subcultures in given societies. In some societies bodily harmful physical force is a regular and an acceptable feature of family relationships; little reduction in family violence, if any, is possible under any conditions in such societies. Some societies define almost all family violence as unacceptable; almost any act of physical force on a family member results in ostracism of the perpetrator. Our own society evidences great subcultural variability in normative acceptability of violence, but the limits of this variability stop short of approaching either extreme. Some significant degree of physical force is acceptable under one or another condition in the family among virtually all types of families.

Given that some idea of acceptable and unacceptable violence is available, the next questions are: When does unacceptable violence occur? And, when does acceptable violence get out of hand and escalate to a degree of force that is not acceptable? These are the essential questions of the issue of the bearing of the normative matrix. The normative matrix can be brought to bear on situations likely to include violence and is thus likely to reduce or eliminate unacceptable violence, under conditions of *surveillance* and/or *accountability*.

Surveillance is a situation in which an individual's behavior is continuously subject to observation by another person who is familiar with the applicable normative matrix — societal or subcultural — and who is in a position to take action if the behavior observed is not acceptable. The action taken can be one of an enormous variety of possible ones. This is the sociological basis of the notion, "sanction." It may be that the observer is in a position to punish, or it may be that an observer's presence results in shame or embarrassment for the perpetrator of the unacceptable behavior. At root, surveillance means the subjecting of one's behavior to constant or almost constant monitoring by an agent capable of effective reaction.

Accountability is a similar notion. Where behavior cannot be directly observed, the notion of accountability means that an individual still stands responsible for certain types of behavior he performs even if those behaviors were not monitored. In regard to family violence, accountability is achieved by structuring things such that if an act of violence does occur information about it is accessible to agents capable of effective reaction even if no direct monitoring was possible. This may mean protection for victims who report violence. It may also mean augmenting the ability of medical and social service people to acquire evidence in cases of suspected abuse of family members.

A word of caution is offered here. The terms "surveillance" and "accountability" are laden with political meaning. The idea of surveillance is not one of posting an FBI agent in every home. The idea of accountability does not necessarily imply opening up every American family to incessant investigations by well-meaning "helpers." On the other hand, the implication is that the contemporary family is low on these two conditions that inhibit violence.

The point to be made is that some fairly "natural" manipulations of the composition and role structure of the family will increase the presence of these conditions, which, in turn, will inhibit family violence. Let us now look at the family.

It is popularly known that the institution of the family has undergone considerable change in the last three or four centuries. In the popular mind this change has been seen as a transition from an extended to a nuclear structure. This is not correct. The western family in most strata has been nuclear throughout the past four centuries and has been so at least since the Middle Ages. The family has indeed undergone change but in the last three or four hundred years the main direction of this change has been toward a radical degree of closure from external influence. This is most visible today in the extreme degree of privacy accorded to the family. In earlier centuries the family was a much more open unit. It was open sociologically and even architecturally. The seemingly fundamental notion of the private family household is in fact an innovation that is but a couple of centuries old. Until recent centuries the home was a small and simple one-room affair for sleeping and perhaps for some meals. It was quite uncomfortable in the cold and in the heat, and it was also infested with rats and bugs. Family members spent most of the day dispersed among the streets, markets, village squares, and the fields. Parental control of children was almost impossible, as children were influenced by a wide variety of village personalities. Work roles occupied virtually the entire nonsleeping time of adults, and so spouses had little opportunity to compose a distinctive interactional pattern among themselves. Under such conditions as these the family was almost totally open to community influence and completely unable to order its internal affairs. In fact there was no internal "social space" that was in any significant degree an exclusive domain of family life. The family was mainly a network of economic and sexual obligations organized under kinship rules and contract marriage.

Even as more familiar forms of households developed, the family was still subject to numerous influences from the outside. As social and economic change raised general standards of living all over Europe and America in the last few centuries, houses became larger and more internally differentiated. The character of work changed, and family members began to spend more time in each others' presence. Concepts of parental guidance of children elaborated, and parents came to be viewed as moral agents in the socialization of their children. A more or less distinctive domain of family life developed, but it was still encumbered by external influence. Religious officials and community administrators had the authority to reach into the home to compel the conformity of family members to officially sanctioned models of moral and popular behavior. The evidence is that this authority was quite frequently exercised. The internal composition of the household itself was laden with "intruders." Records indicated that in the eighteenth and nineteenth centuries the average household's family members were likely to be joined by a variety of servants, boarders, visitors, and, at selected points, slaves, and soldiers. The internal dialogue indeed must have been rich and diversified.

In the most recent century the tendency has been to exclude the intruders and to thereby demarcate a highly private and closed domain of family life. Increasing levels of societal influence has provided, even for the poverty stricken, a form of housing that affords a degree of privacy for family interaction that was unimagined four centuries ago. Increasing secularization has limited the ability of religious officials to intervene in family business of any kind unless the family members choose to allow it. The nature of family life has come to be defined in the popular mind as involving an order of sentiment, intimacy, love, and erotic sexuality that requires extreme privacy if these things are to occur comfortably and properly. The result of these developments is that the contemporary family is, in historical perspective, closed to outside influence to a radical degree. In the face of evidence of widespread violence in families, attempts to develop protective services are currently thwarted by the popularly supported legal presumption that there is no justification for intervening in family affairs without almost prohibitively solid evidence of gross wrongdoing.

This radical degree of closure in the structure of the family renders surveillance and accountability all but impossible. The interior domain of modern family life is virtually walled off from observability of any kind. Whatever order or disorder exists in any given family is almost exclusively a product of its internal processes and goes on unconstrained and unregulated by external influence.   In the absence of surveillance and accountability, unacceptable forms and levels of violence can occur unchecked. The closed structure of the family is responsible for much of the violence that has been found to occur in that institution in modern times.

It seems paradoxical to many analysts of the family situation that such high levels. of violence can coexist with the highly romanticized beliefs about the family. Family relationships are most often conceptualized in terms of images of intimate supportiveness, love between parent and child, conjugal-erotic love between spouses, and so on. These emotional factors of family life have come to be the main and perhaps exclusive function of the family in the past century as other functions, such as economic production and education, have been stripped away from the family. A consequence of the prime focus on emotional expressiveness is that emotional demands are placed on family members that cannot be met. This is the essence of the growing body of literature on the family as a "prison of love." Family violence, in this vein, is an inmate's rebellion. What starts out in a marriage as a prevailing tone of caring, sharing, helping, patience, and good humor, quickly or slowly devolves toward indifference, burden minimization attitudes, and control of temper and anger.   The group of studies of the "crisis of parenthood" indicated that in many, perhaps most, situations the addition of children to the situation compounds the problem by significantly depressing marital adjustment levels and reducing spousal interaction. Where there is a radical absence of surveillance and accountability, emotional sensitivity and irritability can quickly get out of hand and eventuate in explosive violence, and perhaps evolve into a pattern of cyclic violence.

Thus we can see that the content of the normative matrix that is applicable to the family features themes and images that more or less strongly discourage violence. At the same time these themes and images constitute a major dimension of the dynamic that accounts for much of the violence that does occur. Nevertheless, the point to be made is that under conditions of surveillance and accountability the emotional tone of family life is less likely to devolve to the more intemperate levels at which personal control is lost and behavior gets out of hand. Behavior is much more likely to be constrained by the normative matrix, which would predispose toward a positive tone of family interaction, or at least toward the prevention of outward violence and the use of other tension management strategies.

We are now ready to deal with the final question: If the prevailing closed structure of the family supports high levels of family violence because of the resulting absence of surveillance and accountability, how can the structure of the family be opened so as to afford greater surveillance and accountability? As pointed out previously, the objective here is not a matter of police state tactics, rather it is a matter of affecting the composition of households and the permeability of family boundaries to permit any of a variety of natural and familiar types of persons to have a greater degree of presence among family members and a greater degree of awareness of the family's activities. Examples of such natural and familiar types of persons might include parents of one or both spouses, friends, neighbors, etc. Any of these types of persons may exert the desired effect by any of a great number of means, including visits, sharing of meals, participating in leisure activities, being available as a confidante, etc. The main factor behind the value of surveillance and accountability is the fact that an individual is less likely to use violence before an audience. In our normative system losing one's cool, striking others, swinging out in anger, and being the cause of pain and bodily damage to others is viewed as a character flaw. This is particularly so in connection with family members. Most people are reluctant to act in a manner that will result in giving observers the impression that they are deficient in character. Simply involving a friend, or maybe an aged parent, in the family's activities may furnish the needed audience to restrain at least some outbursts of violence in that family.

In more extreme situations the simple presence of an audience at various or even numerous times may not be sufficient. In those cases the audience may have to be omnipresent in order for there to be any effect. While this is a difficult problem, the solution may be the establishment of a three-generation family that includes a spouse's parent as a permanent part of the household to prevent spouse abuse and/or child abuse in the family. Obviously, there is no final and definitive formula. An aged parent might not be an effective audience for these purposes and might only be drawn into the maelstrom of violence as an additional victim. In some subcultures brothers are considered to have continuing responsibility for their sister's welfare. In a situation of wife beating in such subcultures one solution might be to get the victim's brothers involved in the problem as a powerful countervailing force operating on the wife's behalf. In such a situation the brothers are physically able to intervene and perhaps punish the wife beater.

Where audiences cannot maintain surveillance of a violence-prone family, the next best thing is to make family members accountable for unobserved violent acts. This includes protection for victims who report violent acts performed on them from retribution by the perpetrator. But in many, less severe situations the victim may not necessarily need protection. All that may be needed is an opportunity to reveal to someone that violence has occurred. Even where no audience is directly involved, a potential user of violence may be discouraged if it is known that any violent act will ultimately be revealed. A potential wife beater may be deterred if his wife develops a confidante relationship with a friend to whom she will reveal any abuse perpetrated upon her. A potential child abuser may be deterred if it is known that there are daily or weekly physical inspections or examinations at the child's school.

In conclusion, the fundamental point of this chapter is that upon identifying a family in which violence has occurred, or in which violence is likely, the most effective intervention is some manipulation of the composition of the household and/or some manipulation of the conditions under which information about violent acts can flow out of the family. By including an audience in the household or by assuring the ultimate revelation of otherwise hidden acts of violence, the potential for violence becomes subject to greater normative control. These structural manipulations provide for greater surveillance and accountability. The design of specific interventions in specific cases is left to the individual caseworker, family counselor, psychologist, psychiatrist, or other helping professional. This work seeks only to sensitize these professionals to the perspective that family violence has a structural basis, and that this structural basis implies that structural interventions may be the treatments of choice.

Chapter 7

PROGRAMS FOR ASSAULTERS:
Nationwide Trends

Barbara Star

With the possible exception of child abuse, most family vio-
lence-oriented services are designed to aid the victims. We
know very little about the abuser and even less about ways to intervene with abusers to prevent further violence. The knowledge
we do have is tucked away in various local programs that rarely
become known outside of the communities they serve.

During the past five months, thanks to a grant from Levi Strauss
Foundation, I have been locating programs throughout the country that do offer services to the abusers. The intent was not to
locate all known services, but generally to determine the types of
programs that were available and to see what commonalities and
differences existed in the programming between the various categories of family violence. Consequently, I took a broad-based approach and tracked down services by calling agencies listed in various directories, such as family service, child welfare, community
mental health, conciliation courts, juvenile and adult correctional
departments, hospitals, neighborhood centers, and settlements.
In addition, my research assistant and I pursued the names given

The research referred to in this chapter was sponsored by Haven House, Inc., with a
grant from the Levi Strauss Foundation.

by national clearing houses, shelter groups, newsletters, research bulletins, major organizations, and of course, word of mouth.

The main criteria for inclusion in the study was an identifiable program or service, specifically for the abuser, that had been in operation for at least six months. We found that many agencies and organizations had initiated in-service training devoted to one or more aspects of family violence and that victims and abusers of family violence were being integrated into the general client case load of the workers. Even though this type of awareness and integration is what we might strive for in practice, these agencies were not included in this study. For research purposes, we obviously needed to find either components of programs or separate programs specifically for abusers. I was able to locate 110 services sponsored by more than 100 agencies that offer such programs. I have completed most of the initial data collection and will reveal my preliminary findings here.

Let me preface these findings by saying that the people I talked with were among the most dedicated and enthusiastic I have ever encountered. They were willing to talk about what they were doing, wanting to know what else was happening, and were enormously cooperative about sharing their time and knowledge with me. They certainly made me feel that I was involved in a very worthwhile endeavor.

Most of the programs I located dealt with the areas of physical child abuse, sexual child abuse, and spouse abuse. Perhaps of equal importance were the areas in which I could find no separate programs. These involved children who abuse their parents and adults who abuse their elderly relatives. Both of these areas remain mysteries to be explored by adventurous researchers and practitioners.

Among those services I found were twenty-nine that focused solely on spouse abuse; thirty-four that dealt with physical child abuse; twenty-one specifically aimed at sexual child abuse; twenty-five that dealt with both physical and sexual child abuse; two that handled both spouse abuse and sexual child abuse; four that dealt with the areas of spouse abuse, physical child abuse, and sexual child abuse; and five that dealt with the whole gamut of family violence. In general, programs for physical child abusers contained the most extensive variety of services; they were also the oldest.

Many of these programs have been in existence since the early 1970s and offer individual counseling, therapy groups, support groups, parent aides, child development classes, skill training courses, and an array of concrete services. In contrast, services for battering spouses mostly began within the past two years and leaned heavily on short-term groups, marital counseling, individual treatment, and crisis intervention.

There seem to be *three* basic *programming approaches* used with abusers that cut across the various types of family violence categories. The first approach is *counseling* or therapy, which may take the form of individual, marital, family, group, or crisis intervention. The goals are to develop inner awareness, understand the basis of behavior, learn alternatives to current behavioral patterns, identify and label feelings, clarify role behaviors, and enhance interpersonal communication. For instance, an agency in Illinois connected with a juvenile court offers sexual abusers and their families long-term individual therapy, marital counseling, and family therapy. A multidisciplinary counseling center in Colorado is also a long-term treatment resource that focuses on once-a-week marital therapy that deals with the issues of husband-wife communication and self-esteem.

The second approach is *educational*. The emphasis here is on the acquisition of new information and on skill development. Assertiveness training, relaxation techniques, parenting classes, and anger management instruction belong to this model. A family service agency in Rhode Island offers parents an eight-session child management class that follows a prescribed course based on the systematic training for effective parenting approach. A Michigan program for spouse abusers presents a six-session, theme-centered educational group that focuses on marital myths, the dynamics of violence, and the way people communicate. And, a private practitioner in Minnesota uses a cognitive behavioral approach that includes assertiveness training, body awareness, and anger management.

The third approach is *supportive*. Its goal is to reduce or eliminate the sources of stress that increase the likelihood of violent reactions. The more common program components include respite care, homemaker services, case aides who provide concrete services, support, and socialization groups, and parent aides who serve a reparenting function. For example, an Hawaiian social service agency offers a broad-based outreach program using para-professionals who function as homemakers teaching parents budgeting, marketing, and child care skills; lay therapists providing nurturing and parenting to adults; and logistic aids giving transportation and other concrete services to the parents. The Parents Anonymous self-help program provides a well-known model of ongoing group support to potential or actual child abusers. A rapidly growing Parents United program offers similar services to sexual abusers.

Obviously, each of these models overlap to some degree since all may have their therapeutic, educational, or supportive aspects. And, most agencies or organizations offer a combination of these approaches rather than attempting any one in its pure form.

NEWER FORMS OF SERVICES

Because we really don't know yet what works best with abusers, there have been a number of agencies that offer alternatives to the traditional service delivery model.

Coalitions. I encountered several coalitions or consortiums that were established by community agencies to provide a broad-based and integrated network of services to clients. For instance, a group in Indiana concerned with child abuse is composed of a collaboration of thirty-one community agencies that offer a range of services from diagnostic assessment to sponsoring PA groups to providing parent surrogates. Another group in New York state serves a coordinating body that prevents service fragmentation caused by inadequate communication between agencies. Every month they hold team meetings comprised of all people who provide services to a particular family, e.g. CPS worker, therapist, teacher, public health nurse. What makes this group unique is that the parents are also required to be present at those meetings so they can participate, too.

Residential Centers. Another option being offered is residential treatment for the whole family. In California there is a seventy-two-hour residential center that offers a warm, supportive setting in which the family can cool off. And, Tennessee has a two-week residential program that allows time to observe the family's interactional patterns and initiate treatment. A program no longer in existence, but successful as a pilot project, was a four-week program for spouse abusers who were housed in an inpatient unit in a medical center. During their stay the men engaged in assertive skill training, a group that focused on sex-role stereotypes, a coping skills group, physical activities, and relaxation training.

In-home Services. If the client won't come to the service, then the service will go to the client. In-home services are a third option to traditional programming. An agency in Iowa spends at least four hours a week for eight months providing family therapy and parenting meetings. In Kansas, one agency offers an intensive in-home service that gives child management skill training during three to five home visits in the first week, three visits the second week, and then one visit a week for the next 2 to 3 months.

Hotlines Plus. The concept of hotlines is certainly not new, but many are doing a good deal of follow-up with clients, and some are combining crisis counseling with short-term respite care such as emergency babysitting, emergency foster care (overnight or weekend), and parent helpers to help with shopping or apartment hunting.

Family Camp. A California agency sponsors a family camp for twelve families that meets for five weekends during a three-month period. The week-ends are highly structured and include a three-hour parent group on Saturday morning that focuses on the parents early childhood experiences, self-esteem, and self-fulfillment; a three-hour information workshop Saturday afternoon on topics such as nutrition or budgeting; recreational activities on Saturday evening; and a three-hour parent education class on Sunday morning that is aimed at the modification of specific behaviors the parent wants the child to change.

SPECIFIC INTERVENTIONS

I'm glad I only deal with the research part of family violence and not direct service, because you have to be fearless to work with abusers — there can be no beating around the bush, no euphemisms, just straight forward talk and confrontation. This is the consensus of opinion about what works best with assaulters. You have to be willing to deal directly with all aspects of the client's behavior, to counter denials by asking for information, to point out discrepancies, and not to skirt the issue of violence or incest. However, almost everyone said the confrontation should be supportive, not brutal or attacking. The last thing you want to do is engage in a "Yes you did, no I didn't" power struggle with the abuser; it is counterproductive. The purpose of the confrontation is to gain what most practitioners consider a prerequisite to achieving success: the abuser takes responsibility for his or her behavior. It doesn't require a detailed confession or a plea for forgiveness. It does require a willingness to own one's behavior and to take responsibility for the consequences of one's actions.

Supportive confrontation and developing individual responsibility were two of the most consistently mentioned items to my question about what techniques seem to work best with abusers. Most of the responses I received to that question were couched in terms of attitudes, schools of thought, client goals, worker attributes, modalities, and broad-based strategies, as well as specific methods for dealing with abusers.

Groups seem to be the modality of choice throughout the country, either alone or in combination with individual, marital, or parent-child therapy. For example, an organization in Delaware offers a nine-week parent training educational group to help parents deal with stress, express emotions, understand normal child development, communicate more effectively, and resolve conflicts, without resorting to violence. An agency in Ohio offers a two-stage group program for child physical or sexual abusers. Phase One focuses on the adults' emotional needs. Graduates of the ten-week program then may enter Phase Two, another ten-week segment that focuses on behaviors encountered in specific types of parent-child interactions. And, a community center in Alaska provides a twelve-week support group for spouse abusers that deals heavily with breaking sex-role stereotypes.

Whether called therapy or classes or self-help, groups serve several vital functions. First, and foremost, they break the isolation that typifies abusers and their families and provide a rudimentary support network. Many places encourage a buddy system among group members so that people may call each other between group meetings when they feel uptight or want to get out of the house for awhile. Groups also enhance the development of socialization skills. And groups make life a little easier for the therapist by enabling confrontation to be made by and among group members and reducing the number of hours the worker spends with individual clients.

Among the most mentioned worker attitudes that create and maintain effective interventions are being accepting, supportive, and nurturing of the abuser without condoning the behavior. As one program director expressed it, "Everyone has told these people how bad they are — bad parents, bad citizens, bad people." They need someone to be on their side, to share their pain, to point out their strengths, to make them feel as though they are valued members of the human race. It is important to establish a nonthreatening atmosphere to show respect for the person and, especially, to be open and honest with them about their situation. Clients need to deal with realities, not with false hopes and empty threats, about what might happen if they don't cooperate.

But some say that no matter how nice you are, love just isn't enough. People who work with abusers have to be part bulldog. They have to be tenacious and persistent in order to prevent abusers from leaving the program. Even though from the agency's point of view their services are essentially voluntary, abusers are frequently forced to accept treatment as the lesser of several unpleasant options: "Which would you prefer — going to jail, losing your children, or going for treatment? Going for treatment? Oh, how nice! Isn't free choice wonderful?" And even though I am being facetious, because no one really pretends to that extent, nonetheless practitioners are left to deal with people who are less than enthusiastic about seeing them. Agency personnel report needing to be prepared to use aggressive outreach tactics — calling the clients, knocking on their doors, providing transportation, child care, evening and Saturday hours — anything to prevent excuses for not using the service. One worker said, "Sometimes we just have to wear them down until they finally realize we aren't going to go away." All these examples demonstrate the active quality of the treatment being offered. The more traditional insight-oriented therapy, the Rogerian non-directive counseling, and the passive, or as one worker called it the "Uh-hum, tell me about it" model of treatment, have not produced the best results with physical and sexual abusers. Experiential, problem-solving, and behavioral approaches are the ones most often advocated. These approaches require active participation by both the worker and the client. Again, all these approaches overlap to some degree.

The more favored experiential methods include role play, behavioral rehearsal, and the Gestalt empty chair technique. Each of these methods recreate a traumatic, provocative, or troublesome interpersonal situation. They allow the participants to see the flow of events, to reexperience the feelings that accompanied the events, and to change one or more aspects of the situation so that the future outcome in similar situations is more satisfactory. Problem-solving measures focus on a search for alternatives to dealing with both specific and general situations, and they expand the available options for channeling thoughts and emotions. For example, "How else can you discipline your child besides hitting him?" "Whom can you call when you start feeling angry or depressed?" "What would be another way to communicate that feeling?" Behavioral methods most often include cognitive restructuring, modeling, and overt desensitization. They use imagery, self-statements, and emulation to affect change in specific situations.

No matter what approach is chosen, they all share certain common features. Each stresses the importance of *self-awareness* and *self-observation*, i.e. of labeling the feelings and determining under what circumstances they occur. Second, they each slow down or *repeat the interactional process* so that clients can experience the nuances in the exchange. Third, they find the point in the interactional process that *triggers the violence* and use that as the cue or signal that alerts the person to potential danger. Fourth, they *substitute* other *thoughts* and actions for the original ones. And fifth, they *acknowledge* the *changes* that take place in behavior, e.g. workers praise their clients when they use the new ways of interacting.

Be supportive, be persistent, be active in your treatment approach, but also be prepared, at least initially, to give abusing clients and their families a lot of your time. Their lives are chaotic, and they bring that sense of urgency, crisis, and impending doom with them wherever they go. They usually have to cope with many real environmental stresses. Their lives have been filled with people who were unreliable and inaccessible. They need someone who can be there consistently, someone who is available more than a hour once a week, and someone who can help them build some structure into their lives. Workers describe their clients as needy, unable to cope effectively in many areas of functioning, possessing low self-esteem, exhibiting many types of impulse management disturbances, such as overeating, substance abuse, and overspending, as well as poor anger control. Establishing limits, setting goals, and being specific all help to channel clients' energies. Many practitioners find that contracting or mini-contracting and focusing on specific tasks are the best ways to avoid overwhelming their clients and to sustain motivation.

BURNOUT

Every time I asked, "What methods are built into your program to prevent worker burnout?" people just laughed. One man said, "Well, we get drunk a lot." People are very aware of the problem caused by burnout, but consider it one aspect of their program that is not as well developed as they would like. However, only a few said they offered nothing; the majority indicated they attempted some measures. The responses given fell within the categories of support, informational input, variety, and periodic distancing.

Mutual support probably led the list as the most favored method. It includes workers sharing case information, venting frustrations and pent-up emotions, commiserating with each other, giving verbal pats on the back, and reporting moments of success when their clients took another step, even a small one, toward changing the abusive situation. Support also was demonstrated through supervisory availability and by outside case consultation.

Informational input takes the form of in-service training, workshops, and conferences. It does not remove stress as directly as mutual support, although most of the training sessions offer the opportunity to do a certain amount of sharing. Instead it diminishes stress by increasing worker competence. The input expands both the worker's knowledge base and technique repertoire or reinforces the effectiveness of the methods they are currently using, therefore making him or her feel better equipped to handle the situations encountered with their clients.

The concept of variety may not sound like a very sophisticated conceptual element, but it probably offers one of the best long-term measures for preventing workers from coming down with a case of the screaming zonkers. Variety means offering workers change. It can mean an occasional change of job responsibility or holding some administrative or community education responsibilities, in addition to providing direct services to abusers, or having a case load composed of various types of problems instead of only one type. Variety also means flexibility, not always having to adhere to the same routine. Many agencies give their workers the freedom to set their own hours based on their client's as well as their own needs. So a person who goes home at 11 P.M., after spending the whole day dealing with unexpected client emergencies, would not necessarily be expected to start work at 8:30 the next morning, but could begin later in the day or could take compensatory time off.

Periodic distancing maneuvers are those that allow workers to insulate themselves from the demands of the job and not just change what they do, but separate themselves from it completely for brief periods of time. Some groups go on weekend retreats to regenerate their energies, to get in touch with their own needs, and to put things in perspective. Some agencies have liberal vacation and sick leave benefits, and some, in addition, give their workers what they call "mental health days," so a worker can call in and say, "I've had it! I'm supersaturated and my whole body is yelling, tilt! Forget about today. I'll be in tomorrow."

Workers told me that burnout is not something to fear, it is an inevitable outcome of working with clients under stress. The important thing to know is when to leave and plan for it far enough in advance to prevent program disruptions by having trained personnel ready to assume required functions.

ELEMENTS FOR AN IDEAL PROGRAM

Although we may not yet know what works "best" with abusers, let me conclude by pointing to some of the elements that the research suggests are important to include if you are developing a program to intervene in family violence. One element is *stress reduction*. It can be accomplished through a combination of counseling, concrete services, and community support. A second element is *impulse control*, which is achieved by using methods that call attention to the signs of anger and develop alternative actions for channeling feelings. A third element is *education*, such as teaching people what constitutes normal growth and development, normal feelings, and appropriate sex-role behaviors. The final element is *socialization*, which occurs through reparenting, outings, or group interactions that help people learn to like others and enjoy life, and the company of others.

Chapter 8

THE REMEDIES: Rhetoric or Reality?

Robert Sarver

I want to talk about some *way out* kinds of things. To do so, I need to lay some *groundwork* so that you will be prepared to "listen." Then, perhaps, the ideas you are about to read might suddenly emerge as not so "far-out." I want to share some thoughts with you, some basic feelings, about where we are today in the United States, particularly with respect to rights, because what we're really talking about is what people's rights are, the rights of people not to have the "hell beat out of them." Also, the right of people not to have "big brother," the government, reaching in and interfering into their daily activities. Thus, four *groundwork* dimensions to one's individual rights must be noted.

First is the dimension of the individual self. We have been hung up, literally, for at least the past twenty years with the idea of our own individual rights — my having the right to do my thing when I "damn well please." John Knowles, when he was Undersecretary for Health of HEW, made a comment (one of those comments that you and I both wish we had said first), "All Americans say that they have a God-given, inalienable, fundamental, basic, absolute right to smoke incessantly, to drink immoderately, to eat gluttonously, and to engage in sexual frenzy." And woe to anyone who says that I don't have that right or who in any way infringes upon that right. But the other side of the coin is that we also say that,

"Ya'll ought to pick up the tab for any illnesses that I might contact or disabilities that I might catch as a result of my taking advantage of my God-given, inalienable, fundamental, basic constitutional right to smoke incessantly, to drink immoderately, to eat gluttonously, and to engage in sexual frenzy." My response is, "I'm not going to pick up the tab for you. Why should I have to do that? Why don't you pay your own way and stop making me listen to you say, Don't mess with my rights."

A second dimension is that most of us are going to live a lifetime and never get a chance to take advantage of our basic constitutional rights. It's true, we really are. Most of us will never get to take advantage of our rights to have the Miranda warning read to us. That's right! Or take advantage of our right to bail, to a free lawyer, to a trial by jury, or to all the appellate rights. We are going to live a whole lifetime paying for those rights, but never getting to take advantage of them. Only the "hairy-legged hoodlums" get to do that. If this is true — if the majority of us are not going to take advantage of these rights — are we then ready to give some of them up? You know, if we stop this bail "crap," we wouldn't be turning killers loose on society on bail, free to rob another filling station, and free to pay the lawyer's fee. That sounds simple enough.

The third dimension is one's individual responsibilities. Sure, it's easy to say that we have these rights, but we also have concomitant responsibilities. But if you don't live up to your responsibilities, why should we grant you these rights? Live up to your responsibilities or we will take away your rights, except for one big problem: specifically, a substantial segment of our society can't live up to its rights or to its responsibilities, such as children, infant children, and mentally disabled folks, who don't have the capability or the capacity for upholding their share of the load. Then to function in a democracy, shouldn't we be our brother's keeper and our sister's keeper? These two ideas come to mind: taking ownership of responsibility, yet taking care of those who cannot, must be blended.

Finally, the fourth dimension is the limitations of our criminal justice system. A heavy load is placed upon the criminal justice system to take care of our problems. The criminal justice system was founded on the basic premise that it is much, much better, and much healthier to allow ninety-nine hairy-legged, vicious, homicidal, larcenous hoodlums go *scot free* before we would convict one innocent person. All of the benefits of the criminal justice system inure to the defendant, not to the state!

Individual freedom and individual liberty has been the cornerstone of our democracy since its inception. We hold this dear! At the same time, this democratic cornerstone may also be the root of many problems. Perhaps we ought to start thinking in terms of the alleviation of pain and suffering as the cornerstone of our democracy, instead of individual freedom. Perhaps a democratic society ought to center around alleviating the pain and suffering of our fellow citizens. Perhaps, then we wouldn't take advantage of our rights at the expense of others, or step all over the less fortunate people with less opportunity to carry their end of it. Let's illustrate this point: A major problem in this country is our sending mixed messages and double meanings to our kids and to everybody else. When the little one is born, the first thing we do is start telling him to walk: "Get up, walk, walk, walk," and then we tell him to, "Talk, talk, talk." "Momma, Momma," he soon says, then, "Dadda, Dadda." Everybody is so thrilled. He can't say enough, and he can't walk far enough. Then he goes to public school, in which case we then say, "Sit down, shut-up, and learn. Don't talk and don't walk around any more." We tell little ones not to tattle tale: "Don't be a tattle tale on your brother, dear." Then, as you grow up and become a citizen, we say: "It is your civic duty to get under oath to snitch and testify against these folks." We tell children, "Don't be violent, don't be hitting on people," then we legislate the death penalty. We read in the Bible, "Spare the rod, spoil the child" (plus some additional religious fundamentalistic support for violence) and perpetrate violent parenting techniques, all the while utilizing Biblical sanctions to do it. We continue to watch such trivia and violence on television. (I have no question in my mind that violence on television affects the conduct of both juveniles and adults.) We want good parenting role models, and we give instructions: "Obey the law, and do what's right," so when daddy needs some rubber bands or paper clips he brings them home from the office, probably exceeding the speed limit the whole way. We cheat on our income tax because it is the thing to do; everybody does it.

We cheat on our expense account, tell little lies, " 'cause it's just the way it is." We tell our kids, "Don't smoke pot, don't drink booze." You open the medicine cabinet and drugs are all over the place for the alleviation of adult pain, but, "Don't you kids use it." And family members may be found cheating other family members, communicating to the rest of the family, of course, that that's the cool way to live.

One of the things that our society has done is to glorify the use of drugs, especially alcohol. Alcohol and other drugs are taken for the alleviation of pain: "If I can give you enough drugs to alleviate your pain, I wouldn't have to *worry with* you." That's the *United Way* syndrome.

It's true. Write one check a year and you will never have to see a poor person or get near anyone. Just write a check and mail it in and say, "Keep those poor people away from me. I don't want to have to look at them — they're so ugly and terrible." Booze will give you a sense of self-esteem or make you feel bigger and better, worthwhile and loved, and make you seem to want to love, too. Pain will lead you into booze, or maybe it's booze that leads to violence and/or other drugs. Then, again, it may not be a case of alcohol leading folks into violence, but maybe the violence leads us into using those things which make us feel better.

We have a due process in our Constitution of the United States. It requires that folks can't be put away, they can't be deprived of their property, or their liberty, or their lives, without due process, and that's fundamental and basic, and it includes expeditious disposition of cases, both civil and criminal, in our courts involving family violence. If I were a king or if I were the Ayatollah, perhaps I would just order the problem eliminated. But we live in a democracy. We form committees, and we debate, and we carry on about these things, but seldom do we ever get much done and, when we do, we just kind of bungle on through. You're never quite sure, as to what the result is — the result of sinister conspiracy or bureaucratic bungling. One is never really sure. It is within this background — this preamble, if you will — that I now elaborate upon twenty-one overlapping revolutionary ways in which we might change society to grapple with today's problems of family violence.

1. *Children's Divorce.* Our law needs to have substantive and

procedural change to provide for a divorce procedure whereby children can divorce their parents, and vice versa. Why do we force people to stay together when they can't get along, are unwilling to, and incapable of doing so? For example, a sexually abused child may live in a onerous, intolerable situation. If this child runs away and is picked up by the police, she is brought back and labeled incorrigible. Can she not choose to divorce her parents instead?

2. *Teenage Emancipation.* We need to have a procedure in our law for premature emancipation of teenagers. Some sixteen-year-olds are capable, every bit as capable as the reader, of handling his/her own affairs. We ought to be able to prematurely emancipate them upon finding that they are indeed more nearly "adult" than they are teenagers or children or adolescents. This has been done around the country, and now is the time to make it a uniform policy.

3. *Citizenship Grades.* Why not have the courts bestow upon teenagers grades of citizenship, depending upon each one's ability to live up to responsibility. The court could weigh ability not to violate the constituted rights and yet avoid giving them all the responsiblities of democratic citizenship. The procedure would provide for raising up to Grade A and going back to Grade C, again depending on ability and willingness to assume the responsibilities.

4. *Parent Training.* Why not require parent training in our public and vocational schools? I am suggesting, for purposes of discussion, that the three R's — reading, 'riting, and 'rithmetic — are meaningless compared to the fourth R, child-rearing, parenting. We are paying a heavier toll by having a group of citizens who can read, write, and do square roots, yet, don't know how to parent. Let's put emphasis on parenting and families first, and learning how to read, write, and cipher second.

5. *Parenting Privileges.* We are going to have to start viewing parenthood as a privilege and not as a sacrosanct, inalienable right. We already do this right now with driving while intoxicated. The First Amendment of the United States Constitution provides that "one shall not be convicted of any criminal offense without due process" and that burden is on the state or federal government to prove guilt beyond a reasonable doubt. Everybody is presumed

innocent until he is proven, beyond a reasonable doubt, by due process, to be guilty. *But* we have one area where that is not technically true, i.e. driving while intoxicated. If you are picked up for DWI and you have a .10 BAC (blood alcohol content), the presumption is that you are guilty, and you go to court with that presumption. Why is our law for DWI different from child abuse, spouse abuse, etc.? Why shouldn't the law shift the burden of proof and responsibility in cases of child abuse to the parent and take it off the state? Make the parents prove that they are competent and capable of being parents. Of course, this would be after the fact of abuse; once the abuse is in evidence, the burden should shift to the parent to prove that he/she has upheld the child's rights and acted as an appropriate parent. The risk to the parent would then be losing custody of that child. Take the burden off the state!

6. *Ad Litems.* We need to provide a societal extension for every child, every family, and every victim who does not have someone and who suffers from social isolation. A guardian *ad litem* would be appointed where there isn't anyone to check on the child — no grandmother, no aunt, no uncle, no brother, nobody. No one should have to live that way! Our society needs somebody who can represent the individual's interest. If we have to pay, let's pay him or her. As a prison warden, I found it to be very important to make the rounds of that prison everyday so I could see every inmate's face and so I could count the lumps and the bumps, being sure to look at him and see if he had cuts about his face and body (because he's not going to tell you about it). I suggest that our law must provide an advocate *ad litem* for every victim of abuse. When abuse occurs the court would assign an advocate, a guardian *ad litem*. The guardian would stay as an advocate for the victim and would have the authority to further prevent violence.

7. *Parenting Plan.* Every American parent in the United States ought to be required to file an alternate plan, a plan detailing what to do with the children if the parent(s) die or become incapable, or unwilling, to raise their kids. This would create an *alternate plan* and would be an expected part of parenting.

8. *Surrogate Parent Training.* Those called upon to raise children need to be trained. Parenting ought not to be a perfunctory,

rhetorical obligation, but a meaningful obligation. This holds true even for parent surrogates, such as grandparents. (Some of you are probably godparents. I know I am. I didn't see those kids from the day they were baptized till the day they graduated from college: "What is his name again? I'm his godfather." It's perfunctory, it's one of those things, but it doesn't have meaning. Why shouldn't we put meaning into it and make that part of it work?) Parents or parental surrogates/*ad litems* may need financial aid, but I would rather the state provide for financial aid at this early stage than to pick up a later tab for the child's incarceration, or burial.

9. *Permanency Planning.* We have obstetricians, pediatricians, parents, surrogate parents, relatives, day-care center employees, and kindergarten teachers. All of these people have an interest in the development and growth of a child. Why shouldn't they participate actively in it? Why shouldn't we have a burden that they participate actively in it, and not simply sit back and say, "What was that kid's name I birthed a couple of years ago? Where is he now?" We now have permanency planning in most of our states for children in foster care. Why not provide permanency planning for every child born in the United States? Let's plan for that child. Let's not let him sit out there, surviving, and growing, and developing like a game of roulette, at the willy-nilly pleasure of some parents who may not *give a damn* how he develops.

10. *Predetermine Risk Group.* We must have prenatal detection and determination of the population at risk. Hospitals, doctors, and nurses have to take the position that determining the population at risk before the child is born is just as important a part of the "birthing" process as the birth itself. We know the mother, we often know the father, we know the economic circumstances, we know the health, we know the track record. Therefore, we can diagnose likelihood for future problems. We may not always be right, but we will be right significantly more often than not. If we have to, for God's sake, let's err on the side of the child. We must carry parenting skills all the way through from prenatal care, to birthing, to bonding, to preschool. We must stay interested and alert. Doctors and nurses need to be alert to the early warning signs, and when the early warning signs show, we must have procedures to get in there and do something about it.

11. *Family Medical Care.* Every child should have available regular and frequent medical check ups. Many "kids" go through school up to the sixth year and have never seen a doctor. They don't receive any kind of care at all. Nobody looks at them unless they have a broken arm, fractured skull, broken ribs, or worse. We look at them after the damage is done. In Arkansas, as in many states, all children are wards of the state. This is part of the concept of *parens patriae*, i.e. the state is the father of all of its citizens. Following this theory, we ought to be looking in on our kids regularly and effectively.

12. *Family Escrow Fund.* We must provide an alternative course of action for every victim of family violence — an emergency out or an alternative life-style — to meet existing emergencies when and as they arise. One of the things I suggest in this regard is a family escrow fund. One of the duties that falls upon parents is the responsibility to meet the basic needs of the children's food, shelter, clothing, and medical/dental care. Why not also add *response* to this emergency housing plan in cases of domestic violence? Parents would contribute to it, the government would match it, and the total would become the family's social security. The family would receive an incentive not to be a violent family, not to force victims of violence into the situation where that money has to be spent.

13. *National Family Insurance.* An alternative to the family escrow idea would be a type of national insurance. Folks who use the services would pay for them; those who do not use the service would get a "rebate!" Essentially, this could be done through a national insurance program. Everyone would pay a premium. The insurance company pays off when the emergency occurs. Insurance is such an interesting thing. Essentially, one bets against himself when he walks in and says, "Hi there, I think I'm going to be killed, and I would like to buy a policy." The guy looks you over and says, "You look pretty damn good to me, give me the premium." You have made a bet, haven't you? How will you win it? You say, "I'm going to have a terrible accident, and I think I should get some insurance. I'm going to be in the hospital to have surgery, and blood, nurses roaming about my body, have to have enemas, and I'd like to have a policy." "You look pretty good to me, give me the premium." You bet against yourself. In this case,

the payoff is so important, because the payoff provides an alternate living arrangement for the victim of violence; it protects him but it also puts the burden of paying on the family unit.

14. *Tax Incentive.* A good alternative to the family escrow fund would be the tax incentive. We need economic incentives and economic sanctions for people who don't violate our law. If you are a nonoffending family, i.e. a nonviolent family, you would receive a tax incentive for being so. This could be handled through our existing tax structure with Internal Revenue Service. Tax incentives for cooperation could be given for offering parenting training and support services. All we have to do if you are a nonoffending family is to give you a return on some of your money.

15. *Alcohol Tax.* A third alternative to the escrow fund might be further use of the alcohol tax. There ought to be a tax on the wholesale sale of alcohol. (I don't want to put it on the individual drinks, because the individual drinks are too hard to audit.) Earmark the tax for family therapy in the broadest sense of the word. I'm talking now about correction, alcohol rehabilitation, and drug abuse. Let's earmark it on the theory that alcohol, my friends, is not by any stretch of the imagination carrying its fair share of the load for the cost of crime in this country and the cost of pain that is inflicted as a result of its abuse. That's where the money can come from and that's where it ought to be coming from. We should not be dipping into the pockets of little children to make them pay for it. We ought to make the people who drink the stuff pay for it. It's just this simple.

16. *Stop Gamesmanship.* Our laws and our courts must stop playing the games abusers play. We know the games that alcoholics play, and we know the games that battered spouses and children play: they have to play them to survive. We must stop playing this game and we can't accept excuses, nor can we be making excuses for them. We must provide alternate living arrangements for the people who are victims, and we must act swiftly and surely, demanding appropriate conduct from our citizens.

17. *Teacher/Surrogate.* Every prison, every training school, and every youth service center in the United States should provide mandatory parenting training for those people in them. Folks in

prisons, my experience has been, are largely abused people. They were abused as kids, and now they are abusive as adults. They learn to solve their problems through the use of violence, and they use violence on their victims. We must start training them to do something other than to learn to read and write and giving them a low-valued basic occupational skill. My experience has been that if all you do in your prisons is teach people to read and write and give them a basic skill, you end up with erudite highly skilled hoodlums. They too need *some* survival skills.

18. *Family-Oriented Health Care.* All of our existing community health and mental health facilities must structure themselves to meet the needs of the family, including shelter facilities for victims. We need to use what we already have and expand them to meet these kinds of needs.

19. *Family Court.* We need to establish family court systems. Some states already have family court systems — or something that passes for a family court system. But all too many states have a chancery court that takes care of everything. We need a court with trained judges who can handle family problems, including family violence, and we need a court geared to putting all of its energies of money and staff behind the implementation of the family-oriented court's orders. Judges order people to pay alimony; many times they don't do this. They order men and women to pay child support, and the parent simply doesn't pay it. Judges order them not to hit the spouse, and the persecuter then beats the hell out of his/her spouse. The judge orders a protective custody, and *have you ever tried to stop a fist with a piece of paper*? We need to rearrange our priorities when the lives and well-being and health of citizens are at stake. This is a lot more important than a rate case involving a local electric utility, and *it must take priority*! Even big money interests must take a back seat to family needs in our court system.

20. *Rest and Recreation.* In a democracy as great as ours, can't we afford people an opportunity to drop out? We need to allow people the right to just drop out of it, without having to pick up a stigma of laziness, shiftlessness, worthlessness, without being considered a "no-count bum." In the case of one person, who said, "When really I'm not, I'm tired. I'm tired of playing your silly game, I'm tired of breaking my ass to make a living.

Tired of breaking my ass trying to get ahead, I just want to rest a little bit, but I don't want you to put me away, and I don't want you to condemn me forever for it."

We could learn a lot from the Israel kibbutzniks, with their built-in support system — a support system with built-in interchangeable roles, where one can do his share of governing the group being the mayor and where one can take his turn being the janitor. What would it be like if we could all live in a situation where the janitor is every bit as important as the superintendent of schools, and the pay is equal? Synanon, the therapeutic community, once offered that alternative life-style; it gave people a chance to sit back, take it easy, and get some support, some love, and little sense of self-worth and maybe pick themselves up and brush themselves off and start over again. I think we've got to provide this for the citizens in our country who can't live up to the demands of democracy. Freedom and liberty are unbelievably costly, and they take their toll on citizens in our country. A lot of folks can't handle the freedom and need more structure than our democratic society affords them.

21. *Day-Care Structure*. Finally, we need to expand our existing day-care center structure to provide an opportunity for "time out" for mommas and kids. Let's give mom a place where she can go without worrying about the cost, and let's let her take her child down there where he/she is going to get some love and nurturing, some care and a good lunch. Let's give her a break without putting a stigma on her.

As president of the American Civil Liberties Union of Arkansas, I'm concerned about the liberties and the rights of individual citizens and the possibility of abuse when "big brother" starts nibbling into the welfare of kids. There has come a time in the twenty-one years since I graduated from law school where I begin to see the rights of individual citizens clashing. One has to come out on top: one has to be paramount. Lawyers hear a lot about, "You can't make me testify as to the conversation I had with my client because of confidentiality" — a priviledged communication. Social workers, psychologists, psychiatrists, and doctors have the same thing. I have no problems when talking to my law students when they say, "I don't have to testify about this case of child abuse, because I have privileged communication with my client." When it comes to the protection of your right not to testify against your client and the life of that child, the right to privileged communication must be waived. Human life is too great and too valuable to let it go down the drain because somebody is taking advantage of his right not to tell about it.

There is some fear that abuse can happen. This fear is certainly justified, as we know that bureaucrats make many mistakes, "Those lawyers could mess up a two-car funeral." But the point is that we can mess up lots and lots of things. On the other hand, we are regulating much more complicated businesses right now in the United States. It is just another area, another place, where we have to be concerned and not throw the baby out with the bath water. We don't have to always overreact. I think we must make rhetoric a reality. We must start doing something, otherwise twenty-five years from now we are going to be back here talking about these same problems, and the blood will still be flowing in the streets, and heads are still going to get banged, and our prisons are still going to be full. Our youth service centers are going to be full with waiting lists to get in, and we will have accomplished very little or nothing.

In closing, I want to share something that I think is "kinda" pretty. I want to address it to the people out there. I want to address those who suffer from the United Way syndrome, who don't like poor people because they smell bad, who don't like drunks because they're hard to deal with, to those who would rather just go off on their own way: "I was hungry and you formed a humanities group to discuss my hunger. Thank you. I was in prison and you crept off quietly to your chapel in the cellar to pray for my release. I was naked and, in your mind, you debated the morality of my appearance. I was sick and you knelt and thanked God for your good health. I was homeless and you preached to me about the spiritual shelter of the love of God. I was lonely and you left me alone to pray for me. You seemed so holy, so close to God, but I'm still very hungry, and lonely, and cold." Let's all be on the front lines and make some changes!

Chapter 9

HUMAN SEXUALITY CONCERNS IN THE TREATMENT OF CHILD SEXUAL ABUSE AND INCEST

Janet Rosenzweig-Smith

INTRODUCTION

"Sexual abuse of children is a crime that our society abhors in the abstract, but tolerates in reality" states Dr. Suzanne Sgroi in the book, *Sexual Assault of Child and Adolescents*. Experience is beginning to indicate that incest and sex abuse are not really taboo, but talking about them is.

Nicholas Groth states in the same book that, "It is a widely held assumption that (sexual) contacts constitute a risk to the sexually immature child." All too often, adults in a variety of roles seem to take this concept a step further, extending the risk to verbal "contacts" with a child. We find ourselves, whether consciously or not, buying into the myth of the nonsexual child. Talking about sexual issues allows children as well as adults to express fears and concerns and ask questions in a healthy, appropriate fashion.

The purpose of this chapter is to explore some of the human sexuality concerns associated with child sexual abuse and incest.

While the sexual concerns represent but one aspect of treatment, they are too important an area to be ignored.

THE CHILD

What separates child sexual abuse from other areas of child abuse and neglect? For society in general, and children in particular, sexuality is an area shrouded in secrecy. The genitalia are rarely treated in the same manner as other body parts. Visualizing a child engaged in a sexual act with an adult evokes a visceral reaction in the most seasoned professionals. As practitioners we cannot allow ourselves to project our own anxieties onto the child; the task becomes to systematically demystify the genitals through sexual education techniques, appropriate to the child's age. This includes conversing with the child using his/her terms for the sex parts, presenting charts and diagrams, and answering questions. Excellent references for sexuality education for young people can be found in the books *Show Me* for young children and *You* by Sol Gordon for adolescents.

Sex information for all people involved needs to include a clear explanation of the sexual response system as a function of the autonomic nervous system. The point to be stressed is that sexual *arousal* is a reflex, a response to specific stimuli. For a child victim, understanding this helps alleviate some of the guilt and confusion that comes from experiencing feelings that were new and strange. This is applicable to many victims; males are often the victim of fondling, oral sex, and heterosexual intercourse. It would almost be a physiologic impossibility not to be aroused from these acts. The conflict stemming from experiencing new and pleasant experiences while engaging in an act that carries with it one of the worst insults in our language can be debilitating.

A useful analogy in presenting this concept to children is making a comparison to tickling. Once it has been established that a child did experience sexual feelings, explain that when they're tickled in certain ways that they laugh or got goose bumps, and this can be compared to having genitalia touched in certain ways, causing different but still special feelings.

In one sample of 127 incestuous families, 89 percent of father or step-father/daughter cases were characterized as nonviolent. Clinical observations show that many incestuous fathers, while feeling insecure in adult sexual relationships, take special care to gently stimulate their young partners. This can lead to feelings of guilt and confusion for the young girls; if discovery of the relationship is extremely severe and unpleasant, this may facilitate repression of sexual feelings. Childhood sexual experiences handled inappropriately may be a precursor to "anorgasmia" or failure to achieve orgasm in later sexual relationships.

For a young child, the sense of self is still in the formative stages. In order to begin developing a sense of self, infants learn where their bodies end and others, especially mother's, begins. Upon completion of this task, children will begin exploring their own bodies and delighting in the various responses they can elicit. Passing through egocentric phases, children need to feel as if they have control over their own bodies. This is one of the few aspects of egocentrism that is reality based. When robbed of this sense of security of self, the developmental process has been interrupted to the detriment of the resolution of childhood narcissism. Results of this can be seen in the classic incestuous family where the power/authority aspect of family roles becomes confused as the child assumes or attempts to assume a disproportionate amount of power and control. However, the same child may be very unassertive and unable to protect herself in other situations, including sexual.

This leads to the need for stressing the concept of developing "healthy selfishness." Healthy selfishness means learning to protect one's self. Healthy selfishness means accepting the body in all aspects. Healthy selfishness includes masturbation.

Dealing with issues around masturbation is vital to the child. Simply discussing masturbation is useful as an assessment tool in learning something of the child's attitudes toward sexuality. Goals must be set realistically, and while the severely abused child from a very rigid, dogmatic family may not be able to accept masturbation for herself, a first goal might be to have her accept the behavior in others. As therapy progresses in other areas, the child may be able to internalize that she has rights to her own body, and that sexual arousal and orgasm are positive, healthy, and self-reaffirming.

Long-term effects on the sexuality of incest victims are a function of the act and the victims themselves. Being sexually exploited and missing the unconditional love and nurturance so
necessary for parents to provide interferes with the child's ability
to develop trusting and truly intimate relationships. Intimacy is
a necessary component of a healthy, loving sexual relationship.
When a child learns that they can only be loved for what they do
or give, they lose sight of the fact that love can center around
"who a person is." Satisfying lovemaking with a partner then becomes close to impossible. When a child's sexual response system
has been stimulated in a frightening, exploitative situation, the
trauma associated with this can be a precursor to suppression of
sexual desire. Adult women who experienced sexual abuse realize
in retrospect that the guilt and shame associated with the sexual
abuse, concomitant with prevailing sexist and repressive attitudes
of our society, make them easy prey to the "nice girls don't"
stereotype that is supposed to magically disappear with marriage.

THE OFFENDER

Recognizing the child's sexuality is but one issue. Working with
incestuous fathers has revealed a variety of sexual issues, including
feelings of personal and sexual inadequacy, extremely defensive
personalities that render intimacy with an adult partner difficult,
if not impossible, and a lack of knowledge regarding human
sexual functioning, which perpetrates myths, fears, and miscon-
ceptions.

Feelings of sexual inadequacy derive from a variety of sources,
not the least of which is inaccurate information. The statement
that medical studies indicate that the average length of a flacid
penis ranges from 2.5 to 3.5 inches is often met with disbelief.
An incestuous father half-jokingly responded to this in a men's
therapy group by saying, "You mean everyone but me isn't
carrying around twelve inches?"

A concomitant misunderstanding of female sexuality adds to
the sense of inadequacy. When the couple believes that bestowing
orgasms on a woman is the responsibility of the man, this indicates
that the woman accepts little or no responsibility for her own

sexuality. This is problematic, as it is now the male's responsibility for gratification of both of them, and a woman with these attitudes may indeed be anorgasmic. So the male again feels like a failure. Men need to know that all women are different in their sexual responses, that the clitoris exists, that there are no nerve endings inside the vagina, and while intercourse may lead to the husband's arousal and orgasm, it does not necessarily do so for the wife. We need to deal with the fantasy that the penis is the magic wand to orgasm.

Premature ejaculation is not an uncommon phenomenon. While relatively easy to treat in consenting, motivated couples (*see* Masters and Johnson, Singer Kaplan), the man's anxiety that he "just can't do it right" needs to be addressed. As with the child, the man needs to develop a clear understanding of sexual response as an autonomic reflex. As a goal of treatment is to encourage the abuser to accept responsibility for the sexual abuse, it is crucial that they realize that they cannot blame sexual arousal on a child! A corollary to this is the understanding that an erection does not necessarily have to be followed to the nearest vagina; that there are choices to be made once sexually stimulated.

Masturbation is an important issue for the offenders. One client, being interviewed by an overly ambitious, inexperienced counselor (me), got dangerously angry when it was suggested to him that masturbation can be okay and feel good. He absolutely insisted that it was *strictly* a way of dealing with a problem erection. Thus, he indicated a strong feeling that sexuality is intrinsically wrong and enjoying sex was even worse. Marital problems can easily ensue as a function of this attitude. Other clients have bought into the misconception that a man will only have a set number of erections in his lifetime and that masturbation is a waste. This misconception is an indicator to fears of loss of sexual powers, which only adds to the feeling of inadequacy apparent in many offenders.

Masturbation plays another important role. When a client's impulse control and personality have been developed well enough to distinguish between fantasy and reality, masturbation with fantasy can be a way of discharging inappropriate sexual desires. Again, we have to be careful of our own and societal attitudes. A clinician's taboo regarding masturbation, as with other values, should not be apparent when using it as a clinical tool. Masturbation with fantasy is a healthy, appropriate sexual outlet and can richly enhance anyone's sex life. As Shere Hite, Lonnie Barbach, Nancy Friday, and others have indicated, a rich fantasy life can be an integral part of a healthy sexual life and relationship.

Intimacy is also another aspect of a healthy sexual relationship. The ability to develop truly intimate relationships begins with healthy, trusting parent-child relationships. A person learns that exposure of the true self to others will usually result in positive feelings and acceptance. When this task is not completed, developing truly intimate adult personal and sexual relationships is difficult. Assuming that the ego development of the incestuous parent is at a level that does not allow true intimacy with another adult, a relationship with a child can be the least threatening way to feel the need for close human contact. Clinical experience with incestuous fathers indicates that the term "intimacy" bears explaining.

THE COUPLE

A healthy, functioning family is the optimal environment to raise a child; a strong marriage is the backbone to a family; and a fulfilling sexual life is a part of a good marriage. Given this rationale, sexual counseling needs to be provided for the parents in an incestuous family system.

A comprehensive diagnostic interview should include data gathering regarding the sexual relationship. Information is available from The American Association of Sex Educators, Counselors, and Therapists (AASECT) on specific techniques for taking a sexual history. It may not be appropriate to deal with marital sexual concerns until the initial crisis has been somewhat resolved. (A client might really begin to question your priorities if you focus on orgasms while they're concerned with criminal charges being filed.)

Logic implies that the issues of understanding sexuality pertinent to the offender also involve the marital partner. Group counseling can be used to introduce sexual issues and to provide reinforcement through learning that peers experience similar probblems, and couples counseling can be used to integrate the concepts into sexual functioning.

CONCLUSION

As with any other type of clinical treatment, priorities must be kept in order and realistic goals set. Healthy sexual functioning is a desirable goal; non-exploitive sexual relationships are more realistic goals. An optimal goal is for a victim to learn to care about herself and enjoy her sexuality as a healthy, fulfilling part of life. Protecting herself from further sexual exploitation may be a first step.

Treatment of child sexual abuse requires a full complement of treatment services, and sexuality education and counseling should be integrated throughout.

Chapter 10

ALCOHOL PROBLEMS AND FAMILY VIOLENCE:
A Message to the Helpers
Riley Regan

Heavy and not so heavy drinking of "booze" is blamed for so many ills of society, and rarely do we really take a serious look at the specifics. For instance, let's look at murders. We've got some really cold, hard figures for you on the murder victims. We're now finding that up to 65 percent of the murders of murder victims were above legal intoxication standards. This means that there are two individuals out there, both intoxicated, and one is killing the other. Murders just don't generally happen to someone walking down the street. The murder victims are individuals who either know each other and who have had a long history together, or are individuals who frequent a particular bar. Murders often take place outside of drinking establishments between individuals who have known each other. More than two-thirds of the simple assault cases (up to 40 percent of the total arrests in our society) are alcohol-related. This figure is something that many of us are pained with and about which we do not know what to do. Researchers surveying some of the larger adult correctional facilities show that over half of the inmates are there for offenses related to a drinking incident or abusive drinkers. The most recent study in New Jersey showed that 58 percent of the inmate population at one of the long-term correctional institutions could very easily be determined as alcoholic and had been known to the community before they came to the final incident that gave them the long terms. *Most alcoholics aren't involved in committing violent crimes!* Yet the data indicated that many violent crimes are committed by alcoholics. Certainly this gives a basic idea of prevalence of the relationship. Why is there such a discrepancy? Clearly a strong prevalence of alcohol abuse exists in family violence situations yet only 22 percent of the referrals coming into alcoholism systems are from social welfare agencies, which are traditionally involved in the family violence settings. A referral rate of 50 percent would be more on target. This is a figure that is even less than chance. Why is it when we go into the morgue and find 56 percent of the deaths on the highway directly attributable to an individual above legal intoxication do state police records show less than 9 percent of the fatal accidents to be alcohol-related?

Some shocking figures stand out in the state of New Jersey. Most of us talk of HMO's (health maintenance organizations) in terms of the wave of the future. The individual is supposed to be able to go to the health maintenance organization and to take care of all his health needs. However, let's look at some "quick" data that we had in the year 1979: 353,000 patient encounters to HMO's were registered across that state of New Jersey — only 40 were for alcoholism and 2 for drug abuse.

What we are talking about are the human factors involved in some of the more sexy issues, and family violence becomes one of the more sexier issues for us to confront. (There are times when the issue is not really family violence, but just another issue tacked onto the the women's issues, and those of us who are very much interested in this problem have been getting pushed aside.) The family violence field reminds me at times of the alcoholism field —

a field that has set up its own separate identity and its own separate shelters — the feeling that predominates these fields is
that "traditional agencies can't help, so we'll set up our own
separate programs." I begin to get the feeling of isolation, of
fragmentism, and it's almost like revisiting some of the alcoholism fields. We've recently received a grant in my state for
a little more than $300,000 to train social welfare agency per-
sonnel. I think that social workers, psychologists, and traditional people that work in these settings, with a very minimum
amount of effort on our part, can have the gap bridged to the
point that we can involve networks of community resources.
Enough resources to treat family violence already exist in our
community, and I want to take this one step further by saying that we have the same amount of resources available to us
for alcoholism — we just don't apply them.

Ten basic points — ten guidelines — need to be considered by
individuals working in family violence settings who are seeing half
of the clientele that is alcohol-related and who are turning their
heads and not recognizing it. It's really difficult to talk to the
folks about attitudes, because this public health problem affects
so many people and has affected so many individuals personally
that we all have turned our heads and backed away from some of
the major confrontation issues.

1. *Know Your Attitudes about Alcohol, Alcoholism, and the
Alcoholic.* No other substance in our society has been legislated
at the rate and the level that we have legislated alcohol. We're,
perhaps, the most ambivalent society in the world today regarding
drinking practices. We go from the prohibition movement, which
says alcohol is an evil beverage and ought to be banned from our
society, to the drinking pressure placed on an individual that rides
in a car pool. When this group stops off on a Friday night to cash
their checks, tremendous pressure is placed on the individual who
doesn't have a drink with the group: "We don't want any weirdos
in our car pool." There are tremendous pressures to drink and
tremendous ambivalence about drinking practices in our society.

I'm very happy to report that it is against the law to have a
drink in an airplane going over Kansas, and I think you all really

need to know that. But I'm really concerned about the pilot having a drink in an airplane going over Kansas to tell you the truth. (Join a group in a treatment center in our state that has four airline pilots from major airlines sitting around talking about flying 747's in a blackout.) I'm really not concerned about the law that says you can't move your drink from one part of the bar to another without the help of the waitress, that the bar closes at two o'clock in our county, and closes at four in another county. I'd like to measure the kinds of deaths that take place in dashing across county lines and state lines. Right now, based on the substance *alcohol* (and I don't think alcohol causes alcoholism), 9 out of 10 people drink in our society without any difficulty, and 9 percent of the drinkers consume 43 percent of the alcoholic beverages: an extremely high-risk group, very prone to creating massive problems in our communities. In a society that derives billions of dollars from the sale of alcoholic beverages — the greatest source of revenue, next to personal income taxes — very little is put back when considering all the death and destruction that it has caused.

There is a wave of prohibition beginning to sweep the country, sweeping the alcoholism field; individuals are preferring prevention measures through legislation on the substance itself. We're getting very much involved in some emotional battles that are beginning to tear the alcoholism field apart today. One such measure is raising the drinking age to eighty. I want you to know that raising the drinking age to eighty within and by itself is just one very small measure of prevention. It won't do very much unless it's accompanied with a broad-based comprehensive education plan. But I'm very tired of having comprehensive health plans that spend more time teaching a kid how to keep his fingernails clean than teaching a kid about the number one public health problem. I'm tired of programs that are dependent on a particular teacher's attitude who may have a drinking spouse at home, whose father was alcoholic, or who had some very painful experiences with his/her own drinking practices. Certainly this individual is not going to teach with any objectivity in community education programs the need for alcoholism programs related to family violence systems, nor will there be concern about the abusing spouse with a drinking problem when protecting the victim is the concern

because "the alcoholic has a tendency to bring it upon himself."
This wave of prohibition is beginning to stress labeling of alcoholic
beverages. To label any beverage that is above 24 percent absolute
alcohol (48 proof), to begin to limit some of the immediate
availability in order to raise prices and taxes, are very weak public
health efforts.

I'm really tired of seeing people who are in this field with very
blatant drinking problems who come to conferences to display
their drinking problem and who talk about what we are going to
do. It's much more comfortable to talk about drug addiction;
it's much more comfortable to talk about some other system than
to deal with our own drinking practices and to put them into any
kind of perspective. This field really needs to examine some of
its own practices — both personally and professionally — in its
relationship to and use of alcoholic beverages.

Know your attitudes about alcoholism! In 1956 the American Medical Society said alcoholism is a disease, and I guarantee that you won't find too many physicians who really believe this. At a conference the other day with forty physicians
I was told very simply that it is a moral problem, that you can't
help alcoholics unless they want to help themselves, and on
and on. This refutes the stigma attached to alcoholism that says
this is a "moral weakness" and not an illness. We were doing
a training program one time, and we went around the room asking different people their definition of an alcoholic. There was
a nurse in the back of the room who was about to dislocate
her shoulder. We already had about twelve definitions up on
the board, and, I said, "Okay, one more definition before you
break your arm." She said, "My definition of an alcoholic is
my uncle." With this answer she became worthy of a little bit
of research. Out of 200 people, she, unfortunately, was beginning
to state very clearly some of her gut-level feelings that permeated
the whole room. She was a batchelor's degree nurse, had been two
years in the emergency room of that particular hospital, was now
supervisor of nursing in one of the units, and had worked previously in an emergency room in another intercity hospital where 50
percent of the incoming patients had an alcohol-related general
condition: "He was a ne'er do good; we didn't know whether he
was going to kiss us or kick us. I lived with him for about five

years, and the thing that angered me the most about him was that he was an intelligent man — he could have quit — and yet he died in a convulsion." She said that 50 percent of the people who came into the emergency room had this self-inflicted illness and were there in that condition because they wanted to be. She said very clearly that the frame of reference of objectivity that's taught in nursing school, and probably the best of all the professions, had no meaning, or value, because if an individual came to that emergency room with a broken leg and was intoxicated, he was her uncle, and he got the same kind of treatment. If an individual had accidentally wandered into the wrong side of town intoxicated and was beaten up by a group of kids, it was again her uncle. This was the kind of treatment that she was applying in her profession and in her professional relationships. Until one can begin to come to terms with his/her own attitudes about alcoholics personally known — about alcoholic fathers, alcoholic parents, and more importantly, about some of the alcoholics personally reached out and helped and worked with and given your all and been burned in the process — then it serves very little purpose to begin to deal with this issue. We're not talking about the establishment of new resources. I don't think the answer to the 40 referrals out of 353,000 or the 2 percent of referrals in a social welfare agency is to set up a brand new agency, because nobody understands us. I really see the battered wife programs beginning to be just this. And, oh yes, I can speak eloquently about women's issues. I was a token male at a task force on women's concerns, and they beat the hell out of me. I went in there saying what's so different about a woman alcoholic anyway and came out with six new halfway houses in the state just for women: women counseling women. But I get very turned off about people using the women's movement and specific issues in specific groups to do training around alcoholism. Alcoholism is not the result of an individual being discriminated against, either racial or as a woman; it's a much more complex situation than that. I don't want to get into causality of family violence and causality of alcoholism. It's so multiple and complex that I think we waste a lot of time looking for some of the answers in causality and fail to treat some of the major issues.

2. *Learn to Recognize the Alcoholic.* The World Health Organi-

zation gives as a definition that "alcoholism is a chronic, progressive illness where an individual loses control of his/her ability to drink, and that loss of control causes problems with the individual's interpersonal relationship, financial life, and/or with their health." This definition doesn't really begin to talk in terms of how much an individual drinks. There are some studies that indicate that individuals were diagnosed as alcoholic only when their drinking patterns exceeded the drinking patterns of the doctor in charge of the case, and many times these are good definitions. Doctors are an extremely high-risk group for both drug addiction and alcoholism. This definition doesn't say what the individual drinks, as the labeling is one issue. The Senate amendment has decided not to put labels on beer, and the fact is that you just have to drink a little bit more beer in order to get intoxicated. Beer is the number one drug of choice among our teenage population today. The individuals with limited drinking experience and, very clearly, individuals with accidents just waiting to happen are in this kind of relationship. We begin to look for other problems that are more comfortable. It's much easier to treat an individual for lack of self-esteem, and it's much easier to focus on the fact that this individual doesn't have a job, that this persons lives in the intercity, and that if you had all his problems you'd drink too. I've heard that from social workers: "I really didn't want to bring up the drinking because it would screw up our beautiful relationship." I got news for you folks: if he can't give up the drinking, you don't have a beautiful relationship. We've been enablers in this field by not confronting the drinking as a bona fide problem.

With all of the data on alcohol and all of the indicated research on alcohol and child abuse, why are there not more referrals? Because we don't recognize alcoholism as an entity all by itself. We begin to say that if we can get this individual a better job, if we can help them with their mental health problems, and if we can get the family back together, then the identified patient won't drink so much. And I want to say that it's the other way around. If you begin to confront a family with a drinking problem, and deal with the drinking problem, suddenly some of the abusive behavior begins to diminish. The individual finds suitable employment, the education level is increased, and some of the mental aberrations that we've confronted for so long begin to diminish and go away. Alcoholism is very clearly not a mental health problem. One out of ten alcoholics require mental health services the same as one out of ten of the general population.

3. *Confront the Alcoholic.* I'm afraid this is very much tied up again in attitudes. It's interesting to note that at some of the young people's AA (Alcoholics Anonymous) meetings, of which I have had the pleasure of visiting, the kids of previously rehabilitated parents or guardians are now themselves undergoing rehabilitation. Now there is a lot of data, much more than there was ten years ago, that indicates that perhaps alcoholism is inherited, at least some forms of it. But that's not the reason they're there. There is some data that indicates that children of alcoholic homes, once they begin to drink, will very clearly have a four times greater rate of alcoholism, and yet this same group of kids are more prone to abstinence on a lifetime basis. Those kids are in AA groups because the parents know that if they don't push this kid into some kind of treatment it's going to get worse. The professionals on the other hand have sat back and said, "It ain't that bad yet" or "He's too young to be an alcoholic." How many judges have you seen put an individual back on the streets without any kind of referral because "he isn't that bad yet?" We find him going home and killing three kids and his wife in total depression, and we say we could have done something about his depression.

At a recent national meeting we spent five days talking about whether we ought to label alcoholic beverages. On three separate occasions during that meeting, I sat down and talked with a group of people whose prime concern was what are we going to do about so and so who has had a drinking problem for the past twelve years. How are we going to begin to confront the issue with a particular woman who is a leader in this field who now has a drug problem? And you know, not a thing was done, in spite of the blatant display and in spite of the visability, because we had rather been involved in some of the easier issues like primary prevention and labeling bottles. Having personally had a thirteen-year history of alcoholism myself, I have gone to a number of social welfare systems, mental health systems, and a state mental hospital. In fact, one time I had a brother-in-law who tried to commit me to a mental health hospital and, through a comedy of errors, ended up getting locked in himself, with me on the outside! I have a two-year history of heroin addiction; I did a term for armed robbery in California; and I was a fugitive for one and one-half years with a five-to-life hanging over my head. I wasn't a very good robber. I shot myself in my leg while robbing a Safeway grocery store, so don't get the idea I was that much together. I came from a household with a father who drank "alcoholically." One Christmas when I was twelve years old he was beating up on my mother, and I went out and crunched his head with a bicycle pump (they made bicycle pumps bigger in those days). I was furious that night; I couldn't really understand the next morning after he woke up and found that he had a bandage on his head that he couldn't recall what had happened. I can recall saying that I would never drink like him, I'll never be like him, and yet my later drinking practices were almost identical. Now you can say that I learned violence. I eventually married somebody with five kids when I got back in the real world, who themselves had been abused, and have seen first hand some of the alcoholic relationships in family violence. Most frustrating is to see people back off from some of the confrontations that will save their client's life, keeping their focus on the easier work with the victim. People back off from making confrontations with alcoholic clients not only because they don't recognize them, but because their attitudes are so distorted from personal relationships with drinking and clients they have worked with before. The major reason that we, the helping professionals, back off from confrontations with alcoholic clients is that we have a gut-level feeling that says that we can't help these people anyway. You can't help an alcoholic unless they want help.

My message, if nothing more in this very brief presentation, is that you *can* help alcoholics who don't want help. There are ways of moving people into systems; we call it voluntary treatment. (The judge offers him six months in jail and then he volunteers for treatment.)

My concern is with the batterer. When people ask me how are you going to get that individual into treatment, I say, "Well, we

take him over to the corner and we give him the same treatment
he gave his wife and kids, and then after that he's very willing to
get into treatment." I'm saying that you can push an individual
into treatment, and the person can get better. But it is dependent
upon the attitude of the individual making the confrontation.
I'm saying that a confrontation that says "you aren't going to
recover anyway" is not going to be well received and isn't going
to work. Take a look at some of your fellow employees that
you know have a drinking problem, perhaps the principal of
your local school, or the supervisor of your agency. What's your
responsibility in letting that chronic illness continue and pro-
gress?

4. *Recognize that Alcoholism is a Family Disease.* Family therapy is the treatment of choice for alcoholism; I'm sure it is the
treatment choice for family violence. In our case when you can't
get the alcoholic to be involved in family treatment there are
things like Al-Anon and Al-Ateen, and there are group therapy
sessions that begin to deal with the family problems. One of the
real interesting problems is what happens to a family when the
alcoholic spouse suddenly begins to recover. I have had no less
than two patients in private practice — one who actually did it and
one who suggested it — who bought their spouse a bottle of
whiskey (one a bottle of Scotch) to celebrate their first year of
sobriety, because the sudden act of the individual getting well,
forcing the family to recover and take its place as a unit again,
was in itself so disruptive and painful. There are a lot of fringe
benefits in living with a battering spouse. For one thing, you can
martyr yourself to the community. One of the initial things that
I have been impressed by is the token battered wife that I see on
some of these committees. They remind me of the token red-neck
recovered alcoholic who has a life-style and a history such that it
can't really happen to anybody else.

5. *Recognize that the Alcoholic Reality is Different from
Yours.* Once I tried this with a group of people at a state hospital.
I sat down with a guy and said, "Mr. Smith, what would you do if
your wife ran off with your next door neighbor, poisoned your
food, gave you a liver condition, stole your car, cleaned out your
bank account, told a bunch of lies about you in the community
that destroyed your reputation, and on and on," and Smith

looking me in the eye said, "I'd hunt that bastard down unto the
ends of the earth and I'd kill her." Uh-huh, gotcha now. "You
know alcohol has done that to you," and he looked me in the eye
and said, "Well you know alcohol is the only thing I've got left."
You can't argue individuals out of their illness. You can't argue
a family out of this illness, the family will protect and hide without a confrontation. More than a third of the alcoholics in our
society are women, and we are also beginning to see a lot of the
battered wives who are also alcoholic.

But that individual wants to drink like *everyone* wants to. He
wants to be a part of the society that advertises its alcoholic
beverages as something sexy, as something adventurous. It's
painful for me to go to a $350,000 split-level home and have to
sneak into the kitchen to get a drink of water because the host
hasn't included any nonalcoholic beverages at the party. In a
drinking society we begin to say that the alcoholic is weak-willed
and is beyond help, beyond the scope of our agency. I'm saying
that the alcoholic's reality is so screwed up and so centered around
the beverage alcohol that every waking moment for that individual
really clearly relates to this person's existence. We are talking
about taking away the one chemical that allows that person some
feeling of self worth, some feeling in the community, and at the
same time taking away the one beverage that very clearly has disrupted the family and has disrupted the individual's life. And to
hell with "if I had his problems, I'd drink like that, too." If
these are your attitudes, you're in the wrong profession. The
fact is that nobody's life drinking alcoholically is better than
their life without drinking alcoholically.

6. *Maintain Humility*. There is a very fine line between the
"helper" and the "helpee." Nobody knows what causes this illness, nobody knows the perfect treatment for all cases and nobody knows why one person will recover and never drink again or
why another person will end up dying in a convulsion on skid row.
The major resource in our society today, in terms of recovery for
an alcoholic, is still Alcoholics Anonymous. A.A. says that a major
part of this illness, whether physical, mental, or spiritual, is that an
individual recovers through the will of God. You don't have to

believe in God, you don't have to believe in anything, but to see a
family surround an individual that has previously had a major
problem with alcohol, to have seen the disruption, to see the pain,
to see everything begin to diminish and come back together is
spiritual within itself. I think we're very gifted to have the opportunity to work in a field like this, to see people recover, because
watching a family stop abusing and stop the violence is really one
of the rewards that we take part in. But I have not yet seen a
professional in this field who has become capable of doing it on
their own without resources. Nobody denies anything other than
the fact that you give your best and everything you can.

7. *Accept Short-Term Goals.* I have friends, who have worked
for over a year with a particular alcoholic and had that individual
turn around and get drunk, and who say "I will never treat another alcoholic as long as I live." I recall that one of the first patients I ever worked with was from the intercity of Baltimore
(this was in a tuberculosis hospital where 60% of the patients
there were also alcoholic). He'd had polio, he was a diabetic, and
had a club foot. When he drank alcoholically he picked fights
with people who were twice as big as him. He had just about
every strike against him, and I saw this guy stay sober for eight
months and then because of some difficulty go back to drinking.
But during these eight months he was able to set up a little business of his own. In any other illness we are content with short-
term goals: well, next time you'll get to diet, next time you'll
cut down and follow a work regime, next time things will be a
little better." But by not accepting this as a bona fide disease,
we rush for the instant cure, and we get very frustrated when an
individual says, "I'm not alcoholic." The response of the professional is, "You didn't want help anyway," or "I'll spend my
time with people who really want help." If we can begin to keep
individuals from drinking for a couple of months, even though
they relapse, we are on the right track.

8. *Know Your Resources.* There are resources in every community. If you don't know who your state alcoholism or drug
abuse director is, get to know that person. Get to know the
kind of programs offered, read the state plan, and see where it fits
in with you, and find out what is going on at your local alcoholism

information center. Talk to recovered alcoholics, and go to AA meetings. I think going to an Alcoholics Anonymous meeting for professionals is perhaps one of the best learning experiences that you can subject yourself to, and I'm amazed at the number of professionals that go there and come back and say, "I really belong." It's an amazing kind of turn of events. Learn about Al-Anon — the family system that brings individuals in and says we're not here to talk about the problems alcohol is causing you or the problems it's causing me. The Al-Ateen meetings are groups that need tremendous expansion, but they're programs where a kid with drinking parent(s), or a parent who has recovered from their alcoholism, can go and share that experience with other kids who are going through the same problem. The results of those kinds of programs have been miraculous.

9. *Use Your Resources.* This sounds a little redundant, but we stick this in there as a means of saying you can know all the resources in the world, but you may not use them. I've seen police officers, in a state where public intoxication has been decriminalized, pick up a public inebriate, walk by the detox center, and take him to jail, "Because I know what's right for these kinds of people." On one occasion, I walked into a building and asked some people from the mental health association what part of the building the alcoholism information center was in, and, though they knew approximately what part of the building it was in (they had only been there about 8 years), they had never even talked with each other before. The attitude that I talked about that says that you can't help those folks unless they want help themselves begins to permeate your relationship while working with people in this field. We have set up separate problem treatment areas that are fragmented and not coordinated with the rest of the health care and mental health system. This is true for alcoholics, and I'm sure that some of the programs for battered wives are going through some of the same phenomena: "We sure would be awfully worried if we referred somebody to another one of those agencies and they got well." There is a reluctance to send somebody to a family service agency because their philosophy is a little different. There's nothing more appropriate in a community than to have a community professional advisory group that brings

everybody from different settings into focus around some of the similar problems they experience. We're all in this thing together. A study recently in Boston showed that out of sixty-six social welfare agencies, less than half of them knew what the other one did, let alone knew individuals in the agencies. We are rushing into the area of this family violence, which I think is halfway filled with problems of alcohol relationships, and yet only 2 percent of the referrals are coming from those structures, because people would rather see somebody die in their setting than refer that person to another agency that may really help that person. We're talking about a battle of philosophies, a battle for resources, and a battle for visibility. I think we can all live in this field in terms of the resources that are available if we begin to use them, to call on each other, and find out what other agencies are involved in.

10. *Learn More About the Major Public Health Systems.* I've touched briefly on some of the ramifications of it and yet some of you, by reading my ramblings, have now had more alcohol information than we teach in some of the medical schools. One physician told me that the only thing he learned about alcoholism in medical school was how to get a disruptive patient out of his office. We spend more time at one of the major institutions in Baltimore studying about berriberri than about this major public health problem. We did a brief study that showed they had five berriberri patients in that particular year, and all five of them were alcoholics. They said, "Well, we don't really need to talk about the alcoholism."

There's another feeling that predominates that says we already know all there is to know about this illness. However, just some of the very basic didactic materials begin to turn up a lot of gut-level feelings. We are forever in this field beginning to put our trip on everybody else: "Why don't you be like me?" or "Why don't you be the mold of our agency?" Not all child abusers are alike, not all wife batterers are alike, and certainly not all alcoholics are alike. Each individual has some specific "unique" needs that require your attention and require every resource that your agency can localize in the field with limited resources.

Now, I'd like to make three recommendations. First, I'd like to see an increased level of awareness and training about alcoholics among all human services providers, particularly those who help in the war against family violence. Second, I'd like to see the training of professional alcohol counselors who are knowledgeable in the association of family violence and drinking and prepared to take the appropriate, needed referral steps. Finally, we're requiring (and I'd like to see it required) in a number of communities that if there is an alcoholism agency in your community and there's a family violence agency that we very specifically require the formulation of contracts of affiliated agreements that say who is going to do what and to whom and where and whatever. This is very basic and simple. But we're not going to begin to even confront the recommendations that I made, the last three, until the alcoholism field, the family violence field, and the community-at-large begin to have their consciousness raised. We're dealing with a major public health problem that kills far more people than drug abuse or heart conditions and perhaps is our number one killer in our society today. Until we can begin to formalize and get out on the table and discuss our own attitudes and our own actions, we won't take some of those very simplistic recommendations.

(Editor's Note: This paper is a transcription of an extemporaneous presentation.)

Chapter 11
EPILOGUE
Gisela Spieker

The use of alcohol and the use of force within a family are not isolated incidents, nor are they unique to American society. Drinking is associated with the user's perception of self, and force is associated with the individual's perception of the world around him. In some people's minds drinking is the same as drunkenness, while others perceive it as a social convention permitted and encouraged by society. Force, i.e. hitting another person, is perceived as outside of social convention, however, force within the family in some people's minds is desirable behavior. The latter is almost universally accepted when described as "spanking," i.e. force exerted against one's own child. Therefore, both drinking and hitting can be acceptable behaviors, as well as unacceptable behaviors.

DRINKING AND ABUSING

The Historical Place of Alcohol and Family Violence

Universally, societies have been concerned with the excessive consumption of alcohol. The earliest prohibitions are included in the Code of Hammurabi. In the eighth century the Emperor of

121

4

China decreed the number of persons and places allowed to sell alcoholic beverages; the King of England enacted the practice of licensing as a way to regulate ale booths; and King Habim of Egypt enacted the first prohibition laws. Throughout Europe in the Middle Ages we find regulations such as the Act of 1436 in Scotland, ordering the closing of taverns at 9 P.M.; in 1496 the Nuremburg Council forbade the sale of alcohol on Sundays and holidays; and in the regions of Islam and Buddhism faith, abstinence became civil law. During most of early history, laws restricted specific groups of individuals from imbibing, such as judges of the reign of Charlemagne, soldiers during the reign of Gustavus Adolphus of Sweden, Roman women, and young men and women of the Aztecs.

Presumably, the events leading to these early statutes and customs were brought about for health reasons and were definitely due to a lack of job performance. Impairment on the job was first recorded in 2100 B.C. in China when two astronomers failed to predict an eclipse because of drunkenness. Concerns for health are more difficult to ascertain. The fact that in the sixth century Bavaria regulated the amount of daily brandy consumption, as well as King James I of Aragon's edict in the thirteenth century to hospitalize those who exhibited recurring drunkenness, could be considered precontrol legislation. However, it wasn't until the eighteenth century that physicians like Dr. Benjamin Rush of Philadelphia and Dr. Zacharius T. Huszty of Bratislava, Czechoslovakia petitioned for state action against alcoholism, can concern for health be accurately traced.

History makes no mention of the alcoholic's behavior in the home. Physical aggression by the head of the household (male) was condoned by law, as evidenced in the Rules of Marriage compiled by Friar Cherubino of Siena between 1450 and 1481. Although omitted from church historical accounts, the Christian church from the time of Constantine (325 A.D.) has a record of practicing and recommending physical abuse of women. The reformer, Martin Luther, recorded his abuse of his wife Katherine.[1] Such behavior of husband toward wife was further strengthened through the political and economic structure of society. Females were totally disfranchised: they had no voting rights, nor could they own property. In fact, before marriage they were the property of their fathers and after marriage the chattel of their husbands. Political and economic rights for women are phenomena of the twentieth century. While this change has had its impact, for many wives this new independence has not reached within the boundaries of their homes and families.

But how is alcohol abuse associated with violence in the family? The answer might be in such psychological concepts as antisocial personality, passive-aggressive personality, and so on.[2] While these are certainly considerations, these are also basic deviant personality traits found in both the drinkers and nondrinkers, who may or may not abuse their families. To associate alcohol consumption and violence one must remember that alcohol is merely a drug-pharmacological, agent-influenced behavior. Such influence was explained by McClelland in his exploration of the power theory.[3] He determined that there are two different patterns, depending on the personality of the drinker. The p-power theory is a feeling of personal powerfulness, uninhibited, and carried out at the expense of others; the s-power theory is social power, a more altruistic form of power to help others. The s-power theory was found to predominate after two or three drinks; heavier drinking produced a predominance of p-power. It might be possible to consider the p-power to be the predominate feelings among drinkers who abuse their wives and children. The fact that the feeling of "unrealistic" power is experienced influences behavior so that it concurs with the individual's perception of powerfulness. Such perception might well include the use of physical force. To use force against others has its detriments, but to use force against family members is considered within safe boundaries. Family members, except under extreme circumstances, have no way of instigating reprisals. Because the abuser tends to express and experience feelings of guilt once sober, one believes that alcohol might be an excuse for physical abuse, i.e. the feeling of p-power gives a sense of pleasure.

CHAPTER SUMMARIES

The contributors to this book view alcohol abuse and violence from varied perspectives. The points made in this chapter are for the express purpose of finding a common denominator from which to discuss all the other contributions: p-power, complementarity of roles, and stress.

P-Power: Flanzer points to the incidence of abuse towards infants, children, and adolescents. While this is frequently traced to the family of origin, it is necessary to remember that much has to do with complementary roles of marital partners. Even during courtship the alcohol abuser tends to show signs of ill-temper, which may relate to feelings of p-power. Abused women frequently report that during courtship their husbands-to-be were very nice and showed few signs of excessive drinking. In these instances, it is believable that p-power was not experienced. In terms of complementary role relationships, we might consider Conroy's discussion of *self-punishing response.*[4] The female feelings of responsibility provide the male with continuity for experiencing feelings of powerfulness in a very "unrealistic" manner. While the same sense of p-power is not applicable to nondrinkers, the "complementarity of roles" concept may be possible.

Complementarity of Roles: Parson's[5] discussion of the male occupational role within the family as contrasted to the female child-rearing role suggests that boys may face a fundamental problem towards achieving identity: "When boys emerge into what Freudians call the 'latency period,' their behavior tends to be marked by a kind of compulsive masculinity. Aggression toward women, who after all are to blame, is an essential concomitant" (p. 315). It appears then that violence directed toward women and children in a family can be explained from various viewpoints with the same outcome. Although women verbalize their inability to leave home for financial reasons, there is still an amount of self-punishment and/or feelings of guilt (for "having caused the problem") experienced by women who remain in such untenable relationships. Pizzey discussed the inability of women in England to leave their husbands because of the total lack of concern and economic support from the social welfare agencies governed by the legal system.[6]

Stress: Star reflects upon violence as a family characteristic frequently derived from inappropriate marital expectations. Many have said that the practice of "honeymoon" after the wedding ceremony in western society is detrimental to the marriage. Honeymooning is a fantasy much like children's fairy tales: both come to an end unexpectedly. In adult married life the rudimentaries of day-to-day chores often befall women. She may be expected to cook, wash, clean the house, and also hold full-time employment. The stresses derived from expected and perceived new responsibilities are often conflicting and may lead to disagreements between the marriage partners. An individual who has not learned to agreeably disagree may well display behavior unobserved previously by his/her partner. In time, unrealistic expectations and inappropriate perceptions tend to lead to violence in families that are unable to handle stress and express disagreements. As Star points out, such people react on impulse. None of this necessarily points to violent behavior learned in the family of origin.[7,8] Steffen also emphasized that violence needs a complementarity. It is not always derived from the theory of p-power, but more appropriately from the stress theory. A wife whose greetings are, or are perceived to be, nagging, may increase stress to a point where the release in the form of violence seems to be the only natural response. In other words, actions may trigger reactions.

Prevention Implications

Krain's concept of surveillance has a far-reaching effect, in that it provides prevention from within the family structure. As known historically, family violence is not a new phenomenon. It, like alcohol abuse, has no respect for class, status, age, or intelligence. Both abuses predominate and carry a stigma in society, and families like to hide them. However, keeping with Krain's suggestion, violence in the family was less of a problem prior to the industrial revolution. This assumption is based on the lack of violence found in today's extended families of India. The status of women in Oriental societies is frequently equated with that of "outcast" by western society, however, violence is not directed toward women. In western society the family of procreation, (i.e. single family, residing alone) evolved during the industrial revolution. The young men and women left their families of origin to work in the cities. This was the beginning of city life with its own deficiencies. At the same time, distilled beverages were also "discovered." To add to the problem, poverty was experienced in a totally different way. The stress of living in closed quarters, away from family support, made families ripe for the experience of violence. In other words, surveillance has totally disappeared in many families. Over the centuries family structure has changed so as to forget the positive aspects of extended family living, i.e. surveillance.

On the same continuum of surveillance with the family structure is the suggestion by Sarver of more intense church involvement in the affairs of family living. Unfortunately, family life is changing rapidly into more separation. The increase in the divorce rate has confused church leaders as to their role with respect to the family; consequently, the emphasis is on theology rather than surveillance.

Sarver relates appropriately to the lack of concern by legislators and theologians for the violence within families. In fact, the bureaucracy seems to designate that certain groups of people are destined to have a life of violence. For some, there is no opportunity for a life of dignity without fear from within the family. Stress lies not only with the family, but in the lack of support systems.

Regan and Star both relate to the need for a new approach to programs. The approach must be goal-directed to what society wishes to accomplish. If the intent is prevention, then we do not need to focus on treatment. Treatment has been offered with minimal results in both the alcoholism and family violence fields. Treatment is also offered on a separate basis so it does not lead to prevention. Alcohol treatment facilities made feeble attempts to include the entire family, but shelters for battered women exclude the male spouses altogether, which does not allow for cohesiveness and inclusiveness of all family members.

Look to the 1980s and Beyond

Could it be that we are coming full circle? Now that efforts are being made to curb violence in the home, we seem to encounter more violence in the streets. Krain's point was that violence in the street found its way into the home with the development of families. Destruction or deterioration of the family structure, as experienced in today's society, may be a reason for the increase in crime on the streets. One could speculate whether the breakdown of family life is instrumental in the acts of terrorism around the globe.

These speculations may be just that, however, because society has become extremely complex and incomprehensible. With the increase in population, the individual feels more isolation and loneliness. The increase in the sheer number of human beings has brought about differences in life-style that we seem to fail to fully comprehend. I am certainly not proposing to understand or suggest future resolve. Permit me to relate briefly to my own life and explain what I mean.

My childhood was spent on an island country surrounded by the Caribbean Sea and the Atlantic Ocean. The country's total population was two million. Our home was in a pueblo of two thousand. One quarter of a century later, this country has nearly six million people. The pueblo of my childhood has grown to 65,000 with its own international airport providing jet service to the major cities of the world. No wonder the warmth and concern for one another no longer exists.

I grew up not knowing about the concept or the programs of social welfare. Caring for one's neighbor was an assumed responsibility. I never heard a disgruntled word when these responsibilities were implemented. Oh yes, the country of my childhood has progressed. It has three graduate schools of social work and as many medical schools. It obviously has social welfare programs and agencies to implement them. Unfortunately, help can only be given by impersonal strangers who work from 8 A.M. to 6 P.M. five days a week. The agencies close during the noon hours.

One may ask why we have alcoholism and violence. Who is there to be fully involved with one's frustrations, stresses, fears, hopes, and joys? These concepts appear to have been more acutely experienced in our society for the past three decades than previously. Mass communication and rapid transportation make us quickly aware of the perils of other lands and customs of other people. The divisiveness of our society is such that only politicians and professionals speak glibly about togetherness, communication, and relationship, while in fact each family member moves to the next suburb to be "left alone." Is it possible to reverse the trend so as to have closer communion among all people, especially family members?

We are told that in the year 2000 Mexico City will have 15,000,000 inhabitants, and there will be more than 100 cities with a population exceeding 1,000,000. To think that we can return to the days of really caring for one another, to establishing an informal, family surveillance system seems to be a dream "pie in the sky." It is most probable that more controls will need to be exerted to achieve a more harmonious life-style, especially among those residing in the same household. A new approach to an age-old concept, "the family," needs to be brought into focus. I am afraid that I am neither willing to predict such an approach, nor set down limits for it. The idea of governmental interference in family functions is a frightening notion. Let us be forewarned, however, that if we ask for government funding for alcoholism treatment, child abuse treatment, and shelters for the elderly and battered wives, that it may lead to government involvement and ultimate control. Can we really expect tax-supported institutions to be governed totally independent from government control? While this is doubtful, we must look at the bright side of human behavior.

Americans have always functioned so as to provide the best course of action, as well as an independent course of action. Awareness leads to treatment, and from there the entire notion of prevention can be implemented. It is unlikely that alcohol(ic) consumption can be prevented or controlled. What can occur are different expectations for those who drink to excess, thereby reducing violence in the home.

REFERENCES

1. Feucht, Oscar E., and other members of the Family Life Committee of the Lutheran Church (Eds.) *Sex and the Church*. St. Louis: Concordia Publishing House, 1961.
2. Bucky, Steven R. *The Impact of Alcoholism*. Center City, California: Hazelden, 1978.

3. McClelland, D. *The Drinking Man*. New York: The Free Press, 1972.
4. Pfouts, Jane H. "Violent Families: Coping Responses of Abused Wives." *Child Welfare*, February, 1978, pp. 101-111.
5. Parsons, Talcott. "Certain Primary Sources and Patterns of Aggression in the Social Structure of the Western World." *Essay in Sociological Theory*, New York, The Free Press, 1966.
6. Pizzey, Erin. *Scream Quietly or the Neighbors Will Hear*. Stuart Hills, New Jersey: Ridley Enslow Publishers, 1977.
7. Straus, M. "A General Systems Theory Approach to a Theory of Violence Between Family Members." *Social Science Info*, June, 1972 (12), pp. 105-125.
8. Laury, G.V. "The Battered Child Syndrome: Parental Motivation, Clinical Aspects." *Bulletin of the New York Academy of Medicine, 46* (9), 1970, pp. 676-685.

INDEX

131